THE KEY TO
PERSONAL PEACE

BILLY GRAHAM

*This Billy Graham Library Selection special edition
is published with permission from W Publishing Group,
a division of Thomas Nelson, Inc.*

W PUBLISHING GROUP™

www.wpublishinggroup.com

*A Division of Thomas Nelson, Inc.
www.ThomasNelson.com*

Dear Friend,

Nothing in recent history has shaken our world so dramatically as the terrible events of September 11, 2001. We are still reeling from those mind-numbing terrorist attacks, and the future is still filled with uncertainty and fear.

Yet the yearning for peace in our world is but a mirror of an even deeper yearning—a yearning for peace in our souls. And just as the search for world peace often seems frustrating and hopeless, so our search for personal peace often seems doomed to failure. Perhaps this has been your experience.

Is peace in our hearts and minds possible? Yes— and in the pages of this little book I invite you to come with me and discover the key to personal peace for yourself.

In the half-century since I wrote my book Peace with God, *many people have shared with me how it helped point them to the path to true peace. My prayer is that this book, based on* Peace with God *(with excerpts from some of my other writings), will point you to lasting peace—peace with God, peace with others, and peace in your heart.*

Billy Graham

1
THE GREAT QUEST

*You will seek me and find me
when you seek me with all your heart.*
—JEREMIAH 29:13, NIV

YOU STARTED on the Great Quest the moment you were born. It was many years perhaps before you realized it, before it became apparent that you were constantly searching—searching for something you'd never had, searching for something that was more important than anything else in life.

Sometimes you have tried to forget about the quest. Sometimes you have attempted to lose yourself in other things so there could be time and thought for nothing but the business at hand. Sometimes you may even have felt that you were and little pleasure there but finding nowhere to stay that's permanent and satisfying.

Yet inside us a little voice keeps saying, *We were not meant to be this way; we were meant for better things.* We have a feeling that there must be a fountain somewhere that contains the happiness that makes life worthwhile. Sometimes we feel we have obtained it—only to find it elusive, leaving us disillusioned, bewildered, unhappy, and still searching.

There are two kinds of happiness. One comes to us when our circumstances are pleasant and we are relatively free from troubles. The problem is that this kind of happiness is fleeting and superficial. When circumstances change—as they inevitably do—this kind of happiness evaporates like the early morning fog in the heat of the midday sun.

But there is another kind of happiness—the kind for which we all long and search. This second kind of happiness is a lasting inner joy and peace that survive any circumstance. It's a happiness that endures, no matter what comes our way. Oddly, it may even grow stronger in adversity.

The happiness for which our hearts ache is one undisturbed by success or failure, one which dwells deep within us and gives inward peace and contentment, no matter what the surface problems may be. It's the kind of happiness that stands in need of no outward stimulus.

This is the kind of happiness we need. This is the happiness for which our souls cry out and search relentlessly.

Is there any hope for this kind of happiness? Is there any way out of our dilemma? Can we really find personal peace?

Yes! But only if we look in the right place.

I may have the glamour of a movie star or the riches of a millionaire and still not have happiness, peace, and contentment. Why? Simply because I have neglected my soul.

The soul actually demands as much attention as the body. It demands fellowship with God, who made it. It demands worship, quietness, and meditation. Unless our souls are fed and exercised daily, they become weak and shriveled, just as our bodies do without food. We remain discontented, confused, restless.

Many people turn to alcohol or drugs, trying to drown the cries of their souls. Some turn to new sex experiences. Others attempt to quiet the longings of their souls in other ways. Yet nothing but God ever completely satisfies, because the soul was made for God, and without God it is restless and in secret torment.

No one is so empty as he who thinks he is full. No one is so ill as he who has a fatal disease and yet thinks he is in perfect health. No one is so poor as he who thinks he is rich but is actually bankrupt. It is true physically, and it is true spiritually as well.

OUR DILEMMA

CAUSE AND EFFECT

In our bodies, pain and disease go together: Disease is the cause, and pain is the effect. Pain cannot be relieved, of course, until the underlying cause is removed.

We often see the outward effects of physical disease. For instance, when a friend is diagnosed with cancer, we know from experience that we may begin to see such outward effects of the disease as hair loss, physical weakness, and pale skin color. They go together.

Unhappiness of the soul, like pain in the body, is only an effect of a deeper, underlying cause.

Through the years we have raced up various promising paths that we thought would lead to permanent peace and happiness—paths like political freedom, education, higher standards of living, science and technology, fame and fortune, pleasure and power. Sadly, none of them cures our deeper problem—our spiritual sickness.

If it's true that "for every illness there is a cure," then we must make haste to find it. The sand in our hourglass is rapidly falling away. If there is a path that leads to the light, if there is a way back to spiritual health, we must not lose a single hour in finding it!

WHERE ARE WE GOING?

So "Where are we?" you ask. "And where are we going?" Let me tell you *where* we are and *what* we are. We are empty people in a world of empty nations. Our heads are crammed full of knowledge, our standard of living is one of the highest in the world, our bodies live longer than at any time in history, but within our souls is a spiritual vacuum.

We don't know where we've come from, why we're here, or where we're going. We're lost! And we desperately need to find a way out of our dilemma.

But in order to do that, we must first identify the root of the problem.

3
THE REAL PROBLEM

For all [people] have sinned
and fall short of God's glory.
—ROMANS 3:23

SOME YEARS AGO MY WIFE, Ruth, and I visited the Nazi death camp of Auschwitz, located in southern Poland. Here some six million people—both Jews and non-Jews from throughout Europe—were brutally imprisoned and murdered.

We saw the barbed wire, the instruments of torture, the airless punishment cells, the gas chambers and crematorium. Every square foot of that terrible place was a stark and vivid witness to people's inhumanity to each other.

We laid a memorial wreath and then knelt to pray at a wall in the middle of the camp where twenty thousand people had been shot. When I got up and turned around to say a few remarks to the people who had gathered with us, my eyes blurred with tears, and I was almost speechless.

I couldn't help but ask myself, *How could such a terrible thing happen—planned and carried out by a nation that had produced some of the most highly educated people in the world?*

Then I remembered Jesus' words in Matthew 15:19 (NKJV): "Out of the heart proceed evil thoughts, murders, adulteries, fornications, thefts, false witness, blasphemies." And I knew, the real problem is within us—within our own hearts and minds.

OUR DISEASE

The Bible teaches that our souls have a disease. It's worse than any dreaded cancer or heart disease we can face. It's the plague that causes all the troubles and difficulties in the world. It causes all the pain, confusion, and disillusionment in our own lives.

This disease is the most terrible, the most devastating problem in the universe. It has crippled every one of us. It has destroyed the inner harmony of our lives. It has robbed us of our nobility. It has caused us to be caught in an evil and hideous trap.

The name of the disease is an ugly word. We don't like to use it. We don't even like to hear it. But this spiritual disease is the root of all our troubles. All the sorrow, all the bitterness, all the violence, tragedy, heartache, and shame of history are summed up in this one little word. The word is *sin.*

Sin—plain, old-fashioned sin—is what we are all suffering from today. And it won't do any good to try to dress it up with a fancy, more attractive label. We don't need a new word for it. What we need is to find out what this word—the word that describes our deadly disease—means and what we can do about it.

What Is Sin?

We may want to take a light view of sin and refer to it as "human weakness," but God says it brings us death. We may try to call it a trifle, but God calls it a tragedy. We would pass it off as an accident, but God says it's an abomination. We want to excuse ourselves of sin, but God must convict us of it, and He wants to save us from it. Sin is no amusing toy. It's a terror to be shunned! So we must learn what sin is in the eyes of God.

Bible scholars give us five definitions of sin:

First, sin is lawlessness—the transgression of the law of God. The Bible says, "The person who sins breaks God's law. Yes, sin is living against God's law" (1 John 3:4). It is because we have broken God's laws and commands that we are guilty of sin.

Second, the Bible describes sin as iniquity. Iniquity is deviating from what is right. Iniquity includes our inner motivations, the very things we so often try to keep hidden from other people and God. They are the wrongs that spring from our own corrupt natures.

The Bible describes this inner iniquity when it says, "People are tempted when their own evil desire leads them away and traps them. This desire leads to sin, and then the sin grows and brings death" (James 1:14–15).

Third, the Bible defines sin as "missing the mark." Like an arrow missing the target, sin is falling short of the goal that has been set. God's goal is Christ. The purpose of all of life is to live up to the life of Christ. When we fail to follow His example, we miss the mark and fall short of the divine standard. The Bible says, "All have sinned and fall short of the glory of God" (Romans 3:23, NKJV).

Fourth, sin is trespassing. It is putting self in place of God, or trespassing on God's divine territory. Sin is centering your affection on yourself instead of reaching out with your heart to embrace God. Egoism and selfishness are the marks of sin, as surely as theft and murder are. Putting self first may be the most subtle and destructive form of sin, for it is so easy to overlook.

Jesus said, "If people want to follow me, they must give up the things they want. They must be willing even to give up their lives to follow me. . . . It is worth nothing for them to have the whole world if they lose their souls" (Mark 8:34, 36).

Fifth, sin is unbelief. Unbelief is a sin because it is an insult to the truth of God. The Bible says, "Anyone who believes in the Son of God has the truth that God told us. Anyone who does not believe makes God a liar, because that person does not believe what God told us about his Son" (1 John 5:10).

Unbelief shuts the door to heaven and opens it to hell. Unbelief rejects the Word of God and refuses Christ as Savior. Unbelief causes people to ignore the Gospel and deny the miracles of Christ. So, unbelief is sin.

THE PENALTY OF SIN

Our sins may be very obvious and open, or they may be very subtle and hidden. Perhaps we are preoccupied with things that—while not wrong in themselves—have wrapped their tentacles around us and are squeezing out our spiritual hunger. We may be preoccupied with our careers or families or any of hundreds of other things that can dull our appetites for God and His righteousness.

Regardless of what kinds of sins we have in our lives, all sin incurs the penalty of death. Sadly, none of us have the ability to save ourselves from it or to cleanse our own hearts of sin's corruption. And because the pure and holy God of heaven cannot coexist with sin, we are at war with Him.

AT WAR WITH GOD

The greatest warfare going on in the world today is not between nations and countries. It's between us and God. This is the root cause of our spiritual disease.

We may not even realize that we're at war with God. But if we don't know Jesus Christ as Savior, and if we haven't surrendered to Him as Lord, God considers us to be at war with Him. And it would be the greatest tragedy if I didn't tell you that, unless you repent of your sins and receive Christ as your Savior, you are going to be lost.

But that is not what God wants! God doesn't want us to be at war with Him. In fact, the Bible says, "God loved the world so much that he gave his one and only Son so that whoever believes in him may not be lost, but have eternal life" (John 3:16). God wants to save us, and He has provided the way.

A Cease-fire Is Needed

The key to finding peace with God is to stop fighting Him. God has been trying to get through to us for years with the message that He wants to give us peace. Through Christ He said, "My peace I give you" (John 14:27). He wants to give us peace.

But God can't give us His peace as long as we march under the red flag of rebellion. We must stop resisting God! We must no longer shut Him out of our lives. We must stop fighting! We must surrender to the only One who can rescue us from our problem—the God who created us, the God who wants to give us peace, the God who can forgive sin, the God who loves us.

4
WHAT IS GOD LIKE?

Can you understand the secrets of God?
Can you search the limits of the Almighty?
—JOB 11:7

WHO IS GOD? WHAT IS He like? Can we know Him? Can we even begin to understand Him?

If you're asking these questions, welcome aboard. We all have asked these questions sometime, either aloud or in our hearts, for we can't look at the world around us and not wonder about its creation and its Creator.

As a watch must have a designer, so our precision-like universe has a Great Designer. We call Him God. His name is familiar to the whole human race. But what is God like?

The answer is actually quite simple: God is

like Jesus Christ. The reason is because God came to earth in the form of a man named Jesus. He made God visible to us, and He became our Redeemer. When Jesus returned to heaven, He sent the Holy Spirit to live in those of us who believe in Him.

God Reveals Himself to Us

God has revealed Himself to us in the book called the Bible. By reading the Bible carefully and regularly, we can discover what God is like.

As a diamond has many facets, so there are many different aspects of God. With our limited space, we can cover briefly only four of His most significant attributes.

God Is Spirit

First, the Bible declares God to be *spirit*. Once, while talking with a woman at the Well of Sychar, Jesus made this straightforward statement: "God is spirit" (John 4:24).

What image does the word *spirit* bring to your mind? Do you think of a wisp of vapor drifting across the sky? Is *spirit* just a formless nothingness to you? Is that what Jesus meant about God?

No! *Spirit* means "without body." In fact, it's the *opposite* of body. Yet it is just as real as the pages of this book, or more so.

This infinite concept is difficult for us to understand with our finite minds. It is like trying to explain the sweep and majesty and awe-inspiring grandeur of the ocean to a person who has never seen a body of water larger than a mud puddle. How can such a person fathom the bottomless depths, the mysterious life, the surging power, the ceaseless roll, the terrible ruthlessness of an ocean storm or the all-surpassing beauty of ocean calm? How could you make that person believe such a wonder even exists?

God is not limited to body, shape, or boundaries. Because He has no limitations, He can be everywhere at once—He can hear all, see all, and know all.

We can't do any of that, so we try to limit God and make Him like us. We deny His power to do things we can't do. But our saying it doesn't make it so. There is no limit to God! There is no limit to His wisdom, His power, His mercy, or His love.

forgiveness. It was the love of God that sent His Son to die in our place on the cross.

Never question God's great love, for it is as unchangeable a part of God as His holiness. No matter how terrible your sins, God loves you. Were it not for the love of God, none of us would ever have a chance for the future life. But God is love! And His love for us is everlasting! "God shows his great love for us in this way: Christ died for us while we were still sinners" (Romans 5:8).

THE CERTAINTY OF GOD

Whenever anyone asks me how I can be so certain about who and what God really is, I am reminded of the story of the little boy who was out flying a kite. It was a fine day for kite flying; the wind was brisk, and large, billowy clouds were blowing across the sky. The kite went up and up until it was entirely hidden by the clouds.

"What are you doing?" a man asked the little boy.

"I'm flying a kite," he replied.

"Flying a kite, are you?" the man said, looking up. "How can you be sure? You can't see your kite."

"No," said the boy, "I can't see it, but every little while I feel a tug on the string, so I know for sure that it's there!"

Don't take anyone else's word for God. Seek Him for yourself, and then you, too, will know by the wonderful, warm tug on your heartstrings that He is there *for sure.*

The Bible doesn't teach that there are three different gods, but that there is only one God. This one God, however, presents or expresses Himself to us as three distinct Persons. He is God the Father, God the Son, and God the Holy Spirit.

The Second Person of this Trinity is God the Son, Jesus Christ. He is coequal with God the Father. He is not *a* Son of God but *the* Son of God. He is the eternal Son of God—God exhibited in human flesh, the living Savior.

Here's what the Bible says of Jesus: "No one can see God, but Jesus Christ is exactly like him. He ranks higher than everything that has been made. Through his power all things were made—things in heaven and on earth, things seen and unseen, all powers, authorities, lords, and rulers. All things were made through Christ and for Christ. He was there before anything was made, and all things continue because of him" (Colossians 1:15–17).

And Jesus said of Himself, "Whoever has seen me has seen the Father" (John 14:9). He, and He alone, had the power and capacity to bring us back to God. He would have to be the substitute. He would have to die in the place of sinful people. And all this would have to be done *voluntarily.*

How Jesus Lived

Though Jesus was fully man, all the days of His life on earth He never once committed a sin. He is the only sinless man who ever lived. He was examined by His enemies day and night, but they never found any sin in Him.

Jesus lived a humble life. He didn't try to make a reputation for Himself. He received no special honors from people. He was born in a stable. He was reared in the insignificant village of Nazareth. He was a simple carpenter.

And when He began His earthly ministry, He gathered around Him a humble group of fishermen as His followers. He walked among us as a man. He was one of us.

Jesus lived among us so we could see God with our eyes, touch God with our hands, talk to God with our lips, hear God speak with our ears, and live with God in our world. He came so that we could learn how to be like Him—the Son of God.

We, too, can become sons and daughters of God. Jesus has shown us how to live, love, laugh, and be accepted in the eyes of His Father—our Father. And that's not all He did for us.

6
WHAT DID JESUS DO FOR US?

*The Son of Man came to find lost people
and save them.*
—LUKE 19:10

BARABBAS! WAKE UP, BARABBAS! Your big day
has finally arrived."

When the rusty cell door swung open with a
noisy creak, Barabbas shielded his eyes from the
light. He knew why the Roman guards were there.
He had long dreaded this day, for this was his day
to be executed for his crimes.

At least the sun is shining, he thought. *That's
better than dying in the rain.*

But wait. Something was wrong. The guards
were grinning at him oddly.

"What's this, another one of your demented
jokes?" he asked.

"Barabbas, today you are indeed a fortunate man."

"Why, because I'll at least be out of this rotten hole?"

"No," one guard replied, "because we have orders to release you! The governor, Pilate, has freed you and ordered Jesus of Nazareth to die in your place."

The guards removed his chains and, slack-jawed from surprise, Barabbas stumbled out of the prison into the teeming streets of Jerusalem.

He was guilty; he knew it. But he was free! Absolved of all charges, they said. He'd been saved from the death he deserved by some man named Jesus.

Barabbas, overcome by what had happened, must have fallen to his knees on the stony pavement. All he could think was, *Why should Jesus die for me?*

WHY SHOULD JESUS DIE FOR ME?

What a poignant question! Perhaps you're asking it too. The simple but astounding answer is this: *Jesus was born to die for you.* That was His purpose. That was His mission.

Jesus willingly came from heaven to earth to save sinful people like you and me. He came to appease the wrath of our holy God, who was so offended by our sin. And there was only one way Jesus could do it.

When Jesus was born of a virgin, He was born with the shadow of the cross darkening His pathway. From the cradle to the cross, He had one purpose—one mission—to die for you and me.

FORSAKEN AND FORGIVEN

God's holiness demands a sacrifice for our sins. That sacrifice requires death, either for the sinner or a substitute. Christ was our substitute!

It wasn't the vicious spikes that held Christ to the cross—it was the unbreakable cords of God's love that bound Him there. For you! For me! He bore our sins in His body upon the cross.

But the physical suffering of Jesus Christ was not the worst part of His suffering. The deepest suffering of Jesus Christ was spiritual. He felt the final blow of sin and sank to His deepest sorrow when He cried, "My God, why have *You* forsaken me?" The wondrous truth: He was *God-forsaken* so that we could be *God-forgiven*.

He bore my sins in His body upon the cross. He hung where I should have hung. The pains of hell that should have been mine were heaped on Him. The substitution was made. The sacrifice was complete.

Now that the foundation of redemption has been laid, we have the key to unlock the door to peace with God—we, as sinners, must believe in God's Son as our Substitute, our Savior, our Redeemer. We must accept the incredible grace of God: "God loved the world [that's us!] so much that he gave his one and only Son so that whoever believes in him may not be lost, but have eternal life" (John 3:16).

GLORIOUS NEWS!

But Christ doesn't remain hanging on a cross with blood streaming down from His hands, His side, and His feet. On Friday afternoon after His death, He is taken down and laid carefully away in a borrowed tomb. A huge stone seals the entrance of the tomb. And soldiers guard it.

Early on Sunday morning—the first Easter morning—three of Jesus' followers named Mary, Mary Magdalene, and Salome make their way to the tomb to anoint Jesus' dead body with burial spices. But when they arrive, they are startled to find the stone rolled away. And the tomb is empty!

An angel in gleaming white robes is sitting on the stone. He says to the women, "Don't be afraid. I know that you are looking for Jesus, who has been crucified."

And then the angel gives the most glorious news that human ears have ever heard: "He is not here; He is risen from the dead!"

THE FACT OF THE RESURRECTION

Upon that great fact hangs God's entire plan of redemption. Without the Resurrection we could have no salvation.

In actuality, there is more evidence from eyewitnesses that Jesus rose from the dead than there is that Julius Caesar ever lived or that Alexander the Great died at the age of thirty-three. Jesus' Resurrection is a *fact*. It's undeniable. It's historically accurate. And here is what His Resurrection means for us:

First, the Resurrection proves that Christ was undeniably God. He was what He claimed to be—God in the flesh.

Second, the Resurrection proves that God had accepted Christ's sacrifice on the cross, which was necessary for our salvation. "Jesus was given to die for our sins, and he was raised from the dead to make us right with God" (Romans 4:25).

Third, the Resurrection proves that we are reconciled, forgiven, and at peace with God forever. "So as one sin of Adam brought the punishment of death to all people, one good act that Christ did makes all people right with God. And that brings true life for all" (Romans 5:18).

Fourth, the Resurrection proves that our bodies will also be raised and made new in the end. "Christ has truly been raised from the dead—the first one and proof that those who sleep in death will also be raised" (1 Corinthians 15:20). Christ promises, "Because I live, you will live, too" (John 14:19).

Fifth, the Resurrection proves that death will be abolished, and we will be with God in heaven for eternity. The power of death has been broken, and the fear of death has been removed for all who believe. Now we can say with the psalmist, "Even though I walk through the valley of the shadow of death, I will fear no evil, for you are with me" (Psalm 23:4, NIV).

7
FINDING THE WAY BACK

Unless you are converted
and become as little children,
you will by no means
enter the kingdom of heaven.
—MATTHEW 18:3, NKJV

YEARS AGO WHILE I WAS PREACHING in
Hollywood, a group of movie people asked
me to talk to them about religious experiences.
After my address we had a discussion period, and
the very first question they asked was, "What is
conversion?"

Sometime later it was my privilege to address a
group of political leaders in Washington. When
the discussion period started, the first question
again was, "What is conversion?"

In many ways conversion is a mystery, for from

our viewpoint it is both our work and God's work. Our responsibility is to turn to Christ in faith and repentance, turning from our sins and asking Him to come into our hearts by faith. We determine to change the course of our lives, and we acknowledge our inability to do this apart from God's help.

When we turn from our sin and toward God, His part of the conversion mystery is to regenerate or renew our hearts and minds. Then we have truly been converted.

GIVE CHRIST YOUR PROBLEMS

What is troubling you today? Is your heart burdened because of some sin that threatens to overcome you? Are you filled with anxiety and worry about some wrong you have done, wondering what will happen as a result of it?

Listen, friend, you can find the key to personal peace by turning to Christ. Change the direction you are traveling and be converted by the Lord Jesus. As a child of God by grace through faith in Christ, you can give these struggles to Him, knowing that He loves you and is able to help you.

THE KEY TO PERSONAL PEACE

The Nature of Conversion

In order to get to heaven, Jesus said that you must be converted. I didn't say it—Jesus said it! This is not a man's opinion—this is God's opinion! Jesus said it this way: "Unless you are converted and become as little children, you will by no means enter the kingdom of heaven" (Matthew 18:3, NKJV).

True conversion involves your *mind,* your *emotions,* and your *will.* Thousands of people have been *intellectually* converted to Christ. They believe what the Bible says about Jesus, but they have never been really converted to Him in their *hearts.*

Conversion simply means "to be changed." Truly converted people love the good they once hated and hate the sins they once loved. They will even have changed their hearts about God. Where they once may have been careless about God or lived in constant fear, dread, and antagonism toward Him, they now find themselves in a state of reverence, confidence, obedience, and devotion.

Converted people also have a constant gratitude to God, a dependence upon God, and a new loyalty to Him. In other words, conversion means a complete change in the life of a person.

FROM SAUL TO PAUL

A great example of conversion in the Bible is Saul of Tarsus. As a young man he started down the wrong path in life by participating in the killing of God's servant Stephen. Acts 8:1 says that when he died, "Saul agreed that the killing of Stephen was good."

That event began Saul's early career of viciously persecuting Christians. Acts 9 continues his story by saying, "In Jerusalem Saul was still threatening the followers of the Lord by saying he would kill them."

But one day, on the road to Damascus, where Saul intended to arrest and kill even more Christians, "a bright light from heaven suddenly flashed around him. Saul fell to the ground and heard a voice saying to him, 'Saul, Saul! Why are you persecuting me?'"

It was Jesus! Saul had come face to face with the God he had been persecuting. And that encounter turned him around and put him on the road to peace—peace with God.

Acts 9:19–20 says, "Saul stayed with the followers of Jesus in Damascus for a few days. Soon he began to preach about Jesus in the synagogues, saying, 'Jesus is the Son of God.'" He was converted!

Saul's name was eventually changed by God to Paul. His conversion was so complete that even his name had to be different! And Paul became one of the greatest spokesmen for Christ the world has ever known.

How About You?

Perhaps you are ready to change directions, too, and start on the way to personal peace. If so, you are probably wondering, *Where does conversion begin? How can I be converted?*

8
WELCOME HOME

Unless one is born again,
he cannot be in God's kingdom.
—JOHN 3:3

IF I COULD COME AND HAVE a heart-to-heart chat with you in your living room, you might confess, "I am perplexed, confused, and mixed up. I have broken God's laws. I have lived contrary to His commandments. I thought I could get along without God's help. I've tried to make up my own rules, and I've failed. What I would give to be born again! What I would give to go back and start all over—what a different road I'd travel if I could!"

If those words strike a familiar chord in your heart, I want to tell you some glorious news. Jesus said you *can* be born again! You *can* have the fresh start for which you've longed. You *can* become a

boarding pass, and walk to the gate. But if you stop there, you'll never make it to Europe. Why? One thing is lacking: You need to get on board the plane!

To know *about* Christ is not enough. To be convinced that He is the Savior of the world is not enough. To affirm our belief in Him is not enough. To believe that He has saved others is not enough. We really don't believe in Christ until we make a *commitment* of our lives to Him and by faith *receive* Him as our Savior. We have to get on board with Jesus!

Why not get on board *today?* The Bible says, "The 'right time' is now, and the 'day of salvation' is now" (2 Corinthians 6:2). If you are willing to repent of your sins and to receive Jesus Christ as your Lord and Savior, you can do it right now.

How to Begin

You may say, "I really want to be born again, but how do I begin?" I would suggest that you make a list of all your sins. Then confess them to God one by one and check them off, remembering that Jesus Christ has promised to forgive. Hold nothing back! Give them all to Jesus. The Bible says, "If we confess our sins, he will forgive our sins. . . . He will cleanse us from all the wrongs we have done" (1 John 1:9).

Next, ask God to cleanse you from those sins you may not be aware of and to make you more sensitive to hidden sins in your life—wrong motives, wrong attitudes, wrong habits, wrong relationships, wrong priorities. You may even need to make restitution if you have stolen anything, or you may need to seek out someone and ask forgiveness for a wrong you have committed.

In this way you "die to your sins" and share in Christ's death on the cross for you. The apostle Paul said, "I was put to death on the cross with Christ, and I do not live anymore—it is Christ who lives in me" (Galatians 2:20).

Your Response

At this moment I invite you either to bow your head or get on your knees and say this prayer:

O God, I admit that I have sinned against You. I am sorry for my sins. I am willing to turn from my sins. I openly receive and trust Jesus Christ as my

Savior. I confess Him as my Lord. From this moment on I want to live for Him and serve Him in the fellowship of His church. In Jesus' name. Amen.

I believe that Jesus Christ is the Son of the Living God. I commit myself to Him as the Lord and Savior of my life.

_____

Signed

_____

Date

If you sincerely prayed this prayer, my friend, then welcome home! Welcome into the love and fellowship of the family of God.

9
PEACE AT LAST

God will wipe away every tear from their eyes,
and there will be no more death, sadness,
crying, or pain, because all the old ways are gone.
—REVELATION 21:4

ONE OF THE POWERFUL, enduring images that my wife, Ruth, and I have of our early years together is of the ticker-tape parades in New York City celebrating the end of World War II. The war was finally over! And those who had been spared from death by the enemy were jubilant beyond words.

Millions of multicolored streamers and mountains of confetti rained down on the returning heroes, who had valiantly fought the enemy and won. Friends, family, and fellow citizens danced in the streets to express their own happiness and excitement.

Emotions ran extremely high—unfettered joy, exuberant hope for the future, and unvarnished pride in the victors. But the emotion that ran deepest, causing tears to rush down the faces of moms and dads, grandparents, and even stalwart soldiers—from privates to generals—was *relief.*

The war was over! We were victorious. The soldiers were home. And there was peace at last.

Now That You're Home From the War

Now that you're home from your spiritual war with God, you must be feeling incredible relief too. With God's help, you've conquered your enemy, the devil. You've been spared from death by Jesus, who acted as your shield in battle. You've been rescued, renewed, and regenerated by God. What amazing feelings of relief and hope and happiness you must be experiencing now. You have personal peace at last!

Still, as a new believer, you probably have many questions. You may be wondering, *Okay, now what? What happens when we become followers of Jesus?* And that's certainly a legitimate question.

48

Here are some things that automatically come with your citizenship in God's kingdom:

You are forgiven! Just think of it! Every sin you've ever committed, without exception—no matter how terrible or heinous—is gone. Jesus took them all onto Himself, and they were nailed to the cross with Him. They are *forgiven* and *forgotten* by God. You are pure in His eyes. You are saved.

You are adopted! You have become a child of God! God has adopted you as His own beloved child. You're a member of the Royal Family of heaven. You're a child of the King, and nothing can change that.

The Bible confirms it: "You are all children of God through faith in Christ Jesus" (Galatians 3:26). This is one reason why it is important for you to become part of a church where Christ is preached, because there you will be with other members of God's family.

You are justified! The moment you were born again, you also received a new nature and were justified in the sight of God. *Justified* means "just-as-if-I'd never sinned." It is God's declaring ungodly people to be perfect in His eyes. God now sees you through the blood of His perfect Son,

Christ, which washed away your sins. You are pure and perfect in God's sight.

Christ is living in you! The moment you received Christ as your Lord and Savior, through the Holy Spirit He came to live in your heart. The Bible says, "God decided to let his people know this rich and glorious secret which he has for all people. This secret is Christ himself, who is in you" (Colossians 1:27).

From Old to New

Soldiers who came home from World War II discovered that many changes had happened while they were gone. And they had to go through a period of adjustment as they settled into their new lives. In the same way, you can expect certain changes to take place now that you've been born again. And you will have a period of adjustment as you settle into your new spiritual life with God.

First, because Christ now lives in you, you will have a different attitude toward sin. You will learn to hate sin as God hates it. You will come to detest and abhor it, because God cannot coexist with sin. "We know that those who are God's children [that's you!] do not continue to sin" (1 John 5:18).

Second, you will want to obey God. The Bible says, "We can be sure that we know God if we obey his commands" (1 John 2:3). It will become extremely important to you to do what God says is right and to avoid what God says is wrong. The Bible will become your daily companion.

Third, you will strive to be separated from the world you once followed. The Bible says, "Do not love the world or the things in the world. If you love the world, the love of the Father is not in you" (1 John 2:15). And here's why that's so important: "The world and everything that people want in it are passing away, but the person who does what God wants lives forever" (verse 17). Forever!

Fourth, you'll have a new love for other people. "We know we have left death and have come into life because we love each other. Whoever does not love is still dead" (1 John 3:14). God is love. As His children, we must also "be love" to those around us. You will want to pray for others and help them, instead of ignoring or hating them.

Peace in Your Heart

The Christian life is the best way of living. Don't overlook the advantage that a Christian has both now and for all eternity.

Now! Jesus said, "I came to give life—life in all its fullness" (John 10:10). We don't have to wait until we die to enjoy the blessings of being God's child. He promises that, if we live according to His guidelines for happiness, life will be better *now!*

Eternally! "God loved the world so much that he gave his one and only Son so that whoever believes in him [that's you!] may not be lost, but have eternal life" (John 3:16).

What a prospect! What a future! What a hope! What a life! I wouldn't change places with the wealthiest and most influential person in the world who didn't know Christ.

I know where I've come from, I know why I'm here, and I know where I'm going . . . and I have personal peace in my heart. His peace overwhelms my soul! In Christ we are at peace even in the midst of problems and pain. The storm may rage, but our hearts are at rest.

We have found personal peace at last!

10
HEAVEN, OUR HOPE

God will have a house for us. . . .
it will be a home in heaven
that will last forever.
—2 CORINTHIANS 5:1

I WILL NEVER FORGET the last few months of
my mother's life, just before she went to be with
the Lord. During those months she grew weaker
and weaker physically, but her joy and excitement
about heaven grew stronger and stronger!

Whenever anyone went to visit her, they came
away marveling at her radiance and sense of
expectancy. Yes, when she died, there were tears.
But in the midst of them, those of us who loved
her had a deep sense of joy and comfort, because
we knew she was with the Lord.

The Glory Ahead

Death is not the end of the story for you as a Christian either. We are just pilgrims passing through this physical world with its pain and suffering. There is life beyond death! This is the clear-cut promise of God in the Bible.

A young man with an incurable disease was reported to have said, "I don't think I would be afraid to die if I knew what to expect after death."

Evidently this young man had not heard of the heaven God has prepared for those who love Him. For Christians there need be no fear. Christ has given us hope!

Do you have that hope in your heart? Do you know that if you were to die tonight, you would go to heaven to be with Christ forever? You can, if you will trust Christ as your personal Savior and Lord. He said, "Don't let your hearts be troubled. Trust in God, and trust in me. There are many rooms in my Father's house. . . . I am going there to prepare a place for you. . . . I will come back and take you to be with me so that you may be where I am" (John 14:1–3).

For Christians, the grave is not the end, nor is

death a calamity. We have a glorious hope—the hope of heaven.

WHAT IS HEAVEN LIKE?

Heaven will be beautiful. It is beautiful beyond description or imagination! Heaven could not help but be so, because it is the Father's house, and He is the God of beauty.

Look at the world around us. God made it! Wherever we look we are surrounded by amazing beauty. And the same hand that made trees and fields and flowers, seas and hills, clouds and sky, made a home for us called heaven.

It is a place so beautiful that when the apostle John caught a glimpse of it, the only thing to which he could liken it was a young woman on her wedding day. He said heaven was like "a bride beautifully dressed for her husband" (Revelation 21:2, NIV).

Heaven will be happy. Think of a place where there will be no sin, no sorrow, no quarrels, no misunderstandings, no hurt feelings, no pain, no sickness, no suffering, no night, and no death. God's house will be a happy home because there will be nothing in it to hinder happiness (Revelation 21:4).

Heaven will be happy also because it's a place of music and song. The Bible says it sounds like many waters crying, "Hallelujah! For our Lord God Almighty reigns" (Revelation 19:6).

And heaven will be eternal. What will make heaven so delightful? It will be that we shall behold the King in His beauty and see Him face to face. We shall be in the very presence of the living God and His magnificent Son for all eternity. *That* is why heaven is glorious!

Christ will be there with us. He will be the center of heaven. To Him all hearts will turn, and upon Him all eyes will rest. And we will rest secure in His presence forever.

Don't You Want to Go There?

Heaven is such a wonderful place! It's a place of unending peace and happiness. Don't you want to go there? I know I do—and I pray you do as well.

Until that glorious day, let us live for Christ. Let us trust Him. Let us turn to Him in our time of need. And let us joyfully walk hand in hand with our Lord Jesus Christ—regardless of our circumstances—until we join Him for all eternity. That is the road to personal peace!

Jesus said, "I leave you peace;
my peace I give you. . . .
So don't let your hearts be troubled or afraid."
—JOHN 14:27

STEPS TO PEACE WITH GOD

1. RECOGNIZE GOD'S PLAN—PEACE AND LIFE

    The message in this book stresses that God loves you
    and wants you to experience His peace and life.

    The BIBLE says . . . For God loved the
    world so much that He gave His only Son,
    so that everyone who believes in Him may
    not die but have eternal life. John 3:16

2. REALIZE OUR PROBLEM—SEPARATION

    People choose to disobey God and go their
    own way. This results in separation from God.

    The BIBLE says . . . Everyone has
    sinned and is far away from God's saving
    presence. Romans 3:23

3. RESPOND TO GOD'S REMEDY—CROSS OF CHRIST

    God sent His Son to bridge the gap. Christ
    did this by paying the penalty of our sins when
    He died on the cross and rose from the grave.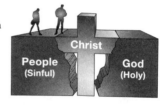

    The BIBLE says . . . But God has shown
    us how much He loves us—it was while we
    were still sinners that Christ died for us!
    Romans 5:8

4. RECEIVE GOD'S SON—LORD AND SAVIOR

    You cross the bridge into God's family when
    you ask Christ to come into your life.

    The BIBLE says . . . Some, however, did
    receive Him and believed in Him; so He
    gave them the right to become God's
    children. John 1:12

THE INVITATION IS TO:

REPENT (turn from your sins) and by faith RECEIVE Jesus Christ into your heart
and life and follow Him in obedience as your Lord and Savior.

PRAYER OF COMMITMENT

"Lord Jesus, I know I am a sinner. I believe You died for my sins. Right now, I turn
from my sins and open the door of my heart and life. I receive You as my personal
Lord and Savior. Thank You for saving me now. Amen."

If you are committing your life to Christ, please let us know!
Billy Graham Evangelistic Association
1 Billy Graham Parkway, Charlotte, NC 28201-0001
1-877-2GRAHAM (1-877-247-2426)
www.billygraham.org

River of Freedom

by Linda Baxter

Cover and inside illustration: Sue F. Cornelison

About the Author

Linda Baxter was born in Cheyenne, Wyoming, and traveled with her military family, finally settling in Tempe, Arizona. She graduated with a degree in elementary education from Arizona State University. Ms. Baxter taught elementary grades in Phoenix, Arizona, and Catshill, Bromsgrove, England.

She lives with her husband, Dave, and three children in Monte Sereno, California.

For information, contact
Perfection Learning® Corporation
1000 North Second Avenue, P.O. Box 500
Logan, Iowa 51546-0500.
Phone: 1-800-831-4190
Fax: 1-712-644-2392
Paperback ISBN 0-7891-5537-0
Cover Craft® ISBN 0-7569-0312-2
Printed in the U.S.A.

Contents

1. On Guard 5

2. Thanksgiving 12

3. Touché 19

4. Monday, December 8, 1941 29

5. A Seat on the Train 33

6. Uncle Jesse 45

7. Suspicion 53

8. Vida 57

9. Parry 67

10. The Tournament 72

11. Catching a Spy 77

12. River of Freedom 84

Epilogue 92

Author's Note 93

Glossary 94

1

On Guard

November 1941

Sasha blinked the sweat from his eyes. He squinted through the screen of the mask. Gasping for air, he tried to fend off his opponent.

He retreated two quick steps. Then he **parried**. His arm ached from holding his **foil** high. His opponent **lunged**. Sasha could not move quickly enough. He winced at a painful jab to his ribs.

The judges raised their hands. The **director** agreed, and another point was counted against Sasha.

"**On guard**," the director called.

Sasha took a deep breath and repositioned. He was ready in a guard position, right arm and foot forward. His opponent advanced.

Sasha knew he should parry, a give-and-take with the blades. Instead he arched forward in a **fletch**. He shot out like an arrow but missed. His opponent deflected Sasha's foil and struck.

"**Touché**!" shouted the director. "**Bout** goes to Harvard."

Sasha groaned and pulled the mask from his face. He shook hands with his opponent and then shuffled over to his coach.

"Bout to Harvard, five **touches** to one," announced the loud speaker.

"Sasha," growled his coach. "You're giving yourself away. He could read you like a book."

Sasha hung his head as a sigh escaped. He ripped open the snaps holding his tight protective collar.

"I was trying to be faster," he said.

The coach continued, "It doesn't matter how fast

you are. You can't fletch on every point. If you're predictable, you'll lose."

"I know," agreed Sasha.

"No, you don't know yet. But you will," assured the coach.

Sasha nodded.

Sasha drew his coat up around his ears. He hurried across the darkening courtyard of **Branford College**. It hadn't snowed yet, but he recognized the crispness in the air. The wind whipped through the barren trees. The winter-browned grass crunched underfoot. Sasha wished he had remembered his hat.

Quickly he dashed up the steps of his dormitory. The bells high above in **Harkness Tower** rang their 6:00 refrain. He gave the heavy oak door a fierce yank. The warmth closed in on him.

Sasha hurried up two flights of steps to the rooms he shared with Keenan. He liked his sophomore dorm at Yale much better than his freshman one. And this year's roommate, Keenan, was more fun.

Sasha reached his rooms at the top of the stairs. He burst into the tiny living room he and Keenan shared.

"I wasn't sure you'd still be here," said Sasha. He shed his heavy coat and rubbed his hands together.

"I'm leaving in a few minutes," replied Keenan. He was just closing his suitcase. Keenan straightened his tall, thin frame.

"I waited for you. Are you sure you won't change your mind?" Keenan asked. "You could still come along. My mom is crazy about you. I think my folks would rather you came home than me," he joked.

Keenan pushed back a lock of straight blond hair and smiled. He shrugged his shoulders good-naturedly. His dove gray eyes crinkled.

Warmed by the offer, Sasha hesitated. Then he shook his head.

"No thanks," he said. "I have to work this weekend. Professor Casey wants me there Friday and Saturday. And I really need the money. Tuition will be due soon, and my scholarship doesn't cover everything."

"Can't you come now and return Friday morning?" suggested Keenan.

Sasha shook his head. "The train is booked solid. I checked. There wasn't a seat left—not even in baggage," he added, smiling.

"But it's okay. It would have been a short visit anyway. Although it would have been worth it for your mom's Thanksgiving dinner. You be sure to tell her that," laughed Sasha.

"I don't know how you can stand to skip Thanksgiving," grumbled Keenan. "It's positively un-American."

On Guard

"I've only had one Thanksgiving in my whole life. And that was last year at your house," Sasha pointed out. "There were no Pilgrims in **Latvia**."

"Well, you have to come at Christmas," insisted Keenan with a chuckle. "If I leave you behind then, Mom won't let me in the front door."

Keenan picked up his suitcase and a huge bag of dirty laundry. Sasha opened the door.

"I'll look forward to it," said Sasha.

"See you Sunday." Keenan smiled and gave him a quick salute.

Sasha watched out of the third-story window as his friend made his way across Branford's square. The silence surrounded Sasha. No one was left on the first long weekend since fall term began at Yale. Sasha sat by the window and stared out into the darkness.

Sasha had turned out the lights hours ago. Sleep wouldn't come. He lay in his narrow bed staring out at the darkened Gothic buildings.

Sasha loved this college. It was built of stone and richly decorated. It reminded him of the old buildings in **Riga**.

The moon hung low in a clear winter sky. Cold blue light crept through the arched window. The small leaded windowpanes glinted.

Sasha rolled over and turned on his small bedside light. He reached into a drawer. The crease lines in the letter were cracked from wear. The delicate paper was rumpled from living in his pocket.

June 4, 1940

Dearest Sasha,

We hope that all of our letters are still arriving. Each time I send a letter, I'll write the last two dates I've written to you (April 17, May 18). If you do the same, we may be able to keep in touch.

We all send our love and hope that you are enjoying your freedom at Yale. I know you will work hard, but don't forget to have fun too.

We are doing fine—really. George's factory is working all three shifts. I rarely see him. He thinks he has found a buyer for his company. We plan to emigrate by the end of summer. Master Heff is confident that he will be able to get the visas to Canada.

Yes, of course we will take Poppy with us. She shakes her head and says that she is too old to sail to a new life. Don't worry, I will convince her in the end.

Larik will start school in Canada in the fall. You won't believe how tall he is. He asks about you often. He has a picture of the two of you in his room.

There is great tension in Riga these days. Some people

*talk bravely of fighting for Latvia's freedom. But we will not be able to stand long against **Hitler's blitzkrieg** if it comes.*

*No one seems to know who would be worse, Hitler or **Stalin**. I am sure those two villains both have plans in mind for us.*

Some refugees from Finland are staying with our neighbors. I cannot imagine the horror of watching bombs fall on your home. I only hope we have not waited too long.

> *Your family sends you all our love,*
> *Your sister Raisa*

Sasha turned out the light. Angrily he plumped his pillow with his fists. He tried to rest but could not keep the faces of his family from invading his sleep.

That had been the last letter. On June 17, 1940, Soviet tanks had rolled into Riga's square. His home and family were held hostage in a world struggle.

Stalin's shadow had loomed for only a year. In the giant tug-of-war, Hitler now controlled Latvia.

German bombs had fallen on Riga in June of 1941. Had they fallen on his home or his family? Were they still alive? Would he ever know?

The pillow captured his tears. Toward morning, he slept.

2

Thanksgiving

The loud banging on his door woke Sasha. The light was blinding. It streamed in from his window. Sasha glanced at the clock and realized he had slept until afternoon.

Thanksgiving

"Hey, Sasha. Are you in there?" called a voice.

Sasha managed a grumble.

"Open the door, man," the voice called.

Sasha woke up enough to recognize Ralph's familiar accent. He stumbled to the door.

"What is it?" sighed Sasha as he opened the door. He tried to shake off his sleepy daze.

"I thought you were going with Keenan for Thanksgiving," said Ralph. He entered, carrying a bag in each hand. Something smelled wonderful.

"I had hoped to, but I have to work," explained Sasha.

"Then it's good I brought your dinner," announced Ralph with a grin. He held the bags under Sasha's nose.

"Smells good," said Sasha. "How did you know I'd be here?"

"I saw Keenan at the train station last night," explained Ralph. He dropped the bags on the table. "I was meeting my aunt and uncle. Keenan said you were staying on campus. I told my mother. She made me drive all the way back from Long Island just to make sure you ate today."

Ralph pulled a roasted turkey leg out of the bag.

"Your family celebrates Thanksgiving?" asked Sasha. Ralph, his mother, and his grandmother had emigrated from Latvia just a few months before Sasha had left. Ralph and Sasha had been good friends in Riga.

"For being a new immigrant, my mother loves everything American. Especially Thanksgiving dinner," laughed Ralph.

"I think she just likes to cook," said Sasha.

Ralph spread the rest of the food on the small table by the window. Turkey, stuffing, and cranberry sauce tempted them. After a hunt, Sasha found two forks.

"I like these orange things," said Sasha. He savored another bite.

"My mother calls those sweet potatoes," Ralph informed him.

They sat back after the food was gone. Ralph groaned and rubbed his large stomach. His round face flushed. He kept his straight black hair cropped short. Sasha stared out the window, frowning.

Ralph asked, "Have you been thinking about your sister?" His blue eyes held compassion.

Sasha shrugged. "How'd you guess?"

"Holidays are the same around the world," said Ralph. "You want to be with your family on those days. Have you heard any more about them? Have you checked with the **embassy** again?"

"I've called the embassy so many times, they know my voice," sighed Sasha. "There's nothing new. There were bombings in and around Riga. That was when the Germans were advancing last summer. One source said that St. Peter's Church had been destroyed," Sasha stated.

"Yes, I heard that," said Ralph.

"There had been many deportations before the Germans got there. Many Russians were 'called home.' One account said that thousands of people were rounded up one night. They were shipped off to **Siberia**," said Sasha. "What about your father?"

Ralph said, "You know how difficult it was for the Jews in Latvia. I'm sure it's even worse now. No one has heard much of anything except rumors. My mother has not heard from my father since the Germans moved in last June."

"Nothing?" asked Sasha.

Ralph shook his head. "She still says he will show up any day, but . . ." Ralph's voice caught in his throat. "If only he had just come with us."

Sasha looked over at the picture of his family sitting on his dresser. "If they had made it to Canada, I would have heard. I'm not sure it makes a difference if the Russians or the Germans hold Latvia."

"It's hard to know who to root for there," Ralph said.

"I also heard that there were battles around **Moscow** this fall," Sasha said. He frowned. His mother had stayed behind in Moscow when he had emigrated to Latvia as a boy.

"I know my mother will be trying to take care of all the wounded," Sasha added. "She'll try to do too much. And what if Hitler were to capture Moscow?" Sasha asked.

"We'll all be in desperate trouble if Hitler takes Russia. We need to pray for a long, cold winter over there. That's what has stopped the Germans for now," stated Ralph.

"Someday, when the war in Europe is over, we'll know what happened to our families. Until then, we both wait," concluded Sasha.

Ralph thought a moment. "I suppose Dieter did me a big favor that day. I would never be here with my mother if he had not blamed that trick on me."

Their friend Dieter had planned a trick on their chemistry teacher, Master Heff. Sasha had been a reluctant participant. A chemical had been substituted to cause a harmless explosion. Ralph had been the one blamed. He had been expelled from school.

Sasha nodded. "Dieter wanted me to enlist in the **Nazi** organization. It was all a plot to get me to join. I will credit him for warning me in the end. Maybe he realized what he was doing before it was too late."

Ralph stood and stretched. He looked out the window.

"It's supposed to snow later," he said. "Do you want to go for a run now?"

"Sure," accepted Sasha. "Just like old times."

Layered in sweaters, Sasha and Ralph ran to the **New Haven Green**. Three small churches pushed their steeples into the evening. No one rested on the park benches. The towering elm trees looked lonely.

Sasha and Ralph jogged through wide streets with

stately homes. Then the boys headed up to East Rock, a viewpoint for the city.

Ralph called to Sasha far ahead. "I never could keep up with you."

Sasha slowed to a walk. He waited for his breathing to return to normal. Leaning against an old tree, he scanned the view of the city. He could just pick out Harkness Tower in the dimming light.

The slate gray river wound through the valley. Sasha turned east. A harbor, lighthouse, and working ships waited in the distance. Long Island Sound disappeared into the coming night.

Ralph joined him, gasping a little. He flopped down on the frozen grass.

"It's pretty here," he stated when he had caught his breath. The winter sun hung low in the sky. It cast deep shadows and hard lines.

"Why didn't you join the track team here?" asked Ralph. "I never understood why you gave up running."

Sasha studied the river below. "I got as far as I could when I made the Latvian National Team. Then the 1940 games were canceled."

"The Olympics would have been so exciting," said Ralph.

Sasha nodded. "Some things just aren't meant to be. Now I have fencing. Maybe I just had to leave that part of me behind. Now I am Sasha Baxter, fencer and American student."

"Why didn't you change your first name too?" asked Ralph. "Maybe Al?"

Sasha had changed his last name from Bausch to Baxter when he had arrived in the United States. He made a face now at Ralph's joke.

Ralph laughed. "Just kidding, Sasha," he apologized.

"You don't play the violin much anymore," said Sasha. "Have you given that up?"

"No, I play for my mother when I'm home. And I play for myself sometimes in the evening. I will never give it up," Ralph assured Sasha.

"Why?" asked Sasha.

"It was the last thing my father said to me. He asked me to play for him," said Ralph.

Sasha just nodded. They sat in silence.

"It's so peaceful," said Sasha after a while.

"It's hard to believe there's a war in Europe," replied Ralph. He tucked his legs under him. "Maybe our families know we're still thinking of them."

"Maybe," said Sasha.

Out of the darkened sky, the first snowflakes fell. More whirled down in the stirring breeze. Quiet surrounded them in a moment of peace.

3

Touché

Sasha stretched out his muscles. He had warmed up by jogging a few laps around the outside of the gym. Then he'd headed to the locker room. There he'd dressed in fencing's traditional calf-length white pants and protective jacket.

Now he sat with crossed legs in the corner. His screen mask rested in his lap. Sasha had a few moments before his lesson. He relaxed, letting his mind wander. But nagging worries soon filtered in.

Quiet moments always caught Sasha thinking of his family. The long-predicted war had begun only weeks after Sasha left his family in Latvia. Hitler had invaded Poland in September of 1939. The German war machine had crushed country after country—Holland, Belgium, Norway.

The world had held its breath that winter, hoping the bad dream would just go away. Then **Dunkirk** had fallen in the spring of 1940. France had surrendered to Germany just as the Soviets swooped into Latvia and its neighbors in June of 1940. England had stood alone. Only a narrow channel and a few brave pilots protected the country. America, his new country, had not chosen sides.

During these trying months, Sasha had endured his own struggles. He remembered the first day he had landed in New York. His ship, the Aquatania, sailed into New York Harbor on a rainy morning. It had been a rough seven-day voyage.

Sasha had only caught a glimpse of the famous statue that greeted so many like him. She'd been hidden from view in the fog.

They had sailed past Ellis Island. The passenger next to him explained that the island was where they had always sent immigrants before. Sasha studied the old buildings as they sailed past. He could almost hear the paint peeling.

The ship had landed at a battered dock. As they walked down the rickety gangplank, other immigrants around him cheered or cried. One old woman had knelt and kissed the ground.

Sasha had just felt lost. He'd wandered through the long lines at immigration. He hadn't been able to understand the English that was shouted at him.

Then his turn had arrived. The old man in a booth looked right through him. Sasha presented his documents, including the precious visa. The immigration officer had glanced, stamped, and pointed to the door.

"I don't understand," Sasha had said. It had been all he could say in English. This was too easy, he'd thought.

The guard had waved him on. Sasha had pushed through the door and found himself in a large waiting area.

"Sasha, over here," someone had called in German. He had searched the crowd and found Ralph.

"Ready, Sasha?" Keenan interrupted Sasha's daydream. His roommate stood over him, foil in hand. Boldly, Keenan swished his foil through the air. He playfully poked at the mask under Sasha's arm.

"Yes, I'm ready," Sasha replied. He jumped up, leaving his memories behind. "I'm going to beat you today."

Keenan grinned. "I hope you do. I can't hold off Princeton all by myself."

They began their lesson.

"Touché!" yelled Sasha. "That was a good point."

Sasha yanked the mask from his flushed face. He drew his sleeve across his brow. Smoothing back his curly brown hair, he grinned.

Keenan smiled as he lowered his foil.

"Good," cheered the coach. "Now you're beginning to understand the strategy. Successful fencing requires a bit of misdirection. You must play with your opponent at first. Try a few **feints** to see how he will react to different attacks. Then change the tempo."

Sasha nodded. "If I can make my opponent think he sees a pattern and knows what to expect, then I have him."

Coach agreed. "Attack in the same line twice."

"Then the third time, disengage and continue the attack rather than parry," Keenan continued.

"Yes," said Sasha.

"I think you'll be ready for the match with Princeton. You must remember to slow down. Throw your opponent off. Wait for the moment."

"Yes, I get it now," agreed Sasha.

"Let's try it again," suggested Keenan.

They stood in ready position, left arm back, foil ready.

"On guard," called Keenan.

Their foils rasped together.

Sasha jogged down the steps of the dorm. He dashed across the wintry courtyard to the main dining room of Branford Hall.

Sasha always liked the dining room. It had a high ceiling and aged wood paneling. He liked looking up at the somber Yale men whose portraits hung on the wall. Even their serious expressions could not quiet the noise of a hundred men eating mountains of breakfast.

Sasha slid into a seat next to Keenan. Ralph looked up from a pile of eggs and toast and smiled.

"Morning, Sasha," Ralph mumbled.

"We wondered if you were going to make it," said Keenan.

"I was working late last night on my English paper," said Sasha. "I always have to spend so much time on English." He smiled slightly.

"I think it's starting to get easier though. I spoke only a few words when I came to the United States two years ago."

"I don't know how you do it at all," said Keenan. "I couldn't go to Latvia and study in a different language."

"You would if you had to," said Sasha. He munched his cold sandwich of ham, salami, and cheese.

"How can you eat that every morning for breakfast?" asked Keenan. "Yuck!"

"It's what I used to eat in Latvia. The cook saves me a little of the lunch meat." Sasha shrugged. "I don't have to do everything like an American, do I?"

"How is the new job?" asked Ralph. "You started with Professor Casey over three weeks ago."

"It's been almost a month now," said Sasha. "Professor Casey is fine to work for. He's so busy that he seldom speaks to me."

"Are you still grading papers?" asked Keenan.

"He had me do that for a few weeks. I did the midterm tests. Now he has me doing these strange puzzles," said Sasha.

"Puzzles?" questioned Keenan.

"What kind of puzzles?" added Ralph with a mouthful of egg.

"Well, they aren't really puzzles. They look like big graphs. I can't imagine what they're for. I have to work out complicated formulas. Then I add the solutions to the graph. I've never seen anything like it," explained Sasha.

"Did you ask him about it?" asked Ralph.

Keenan laughed. "You don't ask Professor Casey much. He doesn't say any more than he has too, even in class," he explained. "I had a calculus class with him last year. He's tough."

"Well, it's better than my first job," said Sasha. "Washing out test tubes in the biology lab was awful. I'll do puzzles until I graduate. I know I'll have to work until then. I don't know what I would have done without the scholarship committee's help."

"Did you ever hear more from your bank in Paris?" asked Ralph.

"Hitler doesn't care whose money he takes," said Sasha. "My family thought my school money would be safe in France. I think it's gone for good."

"Who could have guessed that France would fall to the Germans so quickly?" Ralph asked.

Sasha crammed the last two bites into his mouth. He waved good-bye to his friends.

"See you at the tournament," said Keenan.

Sasha nodded.

Sasha knew he would compete next. He fidgeted nervously with his mask. His name echoed over the loudspeaker.

Sasha picked up his foil and stepped onto the long mat. His opponent stepped forward and carefully studied Sasha. Sasha pulled on his heavy protective glove. He tested the weight of his foil, lightly balancing it in his fingers.

Keenan gave Sasha a thumbs-up sign from across the **salle**. Sasha stood at attention. The director instructed him and his opponent.

Sasha formally saluted the director and then his opponent with his foil. He placed his mask over his face. Then he positioned himself with his foil extended in his right hand. His left arm was back and arched behind.

"On guard!" shouted the director. "Ready, fence."

Sasha focused on the hilt of his challenger's foil. They edged forward and back, eyeing each other warily. Sasha waited for the first attack.

The two men moved closer. They lightly touched the centers of their foils. Testing each other, they attacked and parried. Their foils rasped and clattered together. Sasha kept his movements very small, always guarding.

Then Sasha lunged. The coiled strength in his back leg propelled his front foot forward. His opponent quickly parried and retreated. Sasha recovered. He tried for a touch on the shoulder but felt the quick jab of the foil on his side.

Touché

The four judges raised their hands. The director called, "Touché."

"Sasha, watch for that defense. He's weak to the left," coached Keenan.

Sasha nodded. The director called, "One point to Princeton. On guard."

The fencers began again. Sasha decided to wait. He would get his opponent off balance. When his opponent lunged, Sasha feinted right twice and then moved back and to the left. Then he slipped his blade under his opponent's parry to free himself. His opponent's defense left him wide open. Sasha lunged and scored.

They battled on. They moved up and down the long, narrow strip. Attack, parry, retreat.

The next points were shared between them. They were tied four to four. One point to go.

Sasha's face dripped with sweat. The high, tight collar choked him. His protective jacket felt heavy.

"One more point," whispered Sasha to himself. "I want this."

Sasha forced himself to concentrate. Watch the hilt, not the point. I can be sneaky, he told himself.

His opponent lunged and Sasha retreated. Sasha parried skillfully, staying just out of reach of the foil. He retreated from another lunge.

For a moment, their blades tangled as their foils pressed together. They finally broke apart.

Then Sasha's challenger lunged a third time. He expected another retreat. Sasha stepped with his parry and then **riposted**. He yelled "touché" as his foil arched into his opponent's back.

The judges ruled. "Touché. That is bout to Yale," called the director.

Sasha removed his mask. He saluted the director and his opponent. Then he left the strip.

Keenan hooted as Sasha pulled off his gloves and loosened his high collar. "Great job, Sasha."

Sasha smiled.

"You'll get them every time with that move," said Keenan.

4

Monday, December 8, 1941

Keenan rushed into Sasha's room. "Have you heard? You won't believe it. Yesterday Pearl Harbor was bombed. It was just on the radio," he said.

"What is Pearl Harbor?" asked Sasha. He looked up from working on his next English paper.

"You know, the naval base in Hawaii," explained Keenan.

"What would the Germans want with Hawaii?" Sasha asked, still confused.

A sharp rap at the door brought Ralph dashing into their room.

"Did you hear?" asked Ralph. "We'll be at war with Japan. **Roosevelt** is going to be on the radio in a few minutes. Did you see the newspaper?"

Keenan nodded. "I just told Sasha. Can you believe it? And **Hirohito** has been negotiating with Roosevelt for weeks." He turned to Sasha.

"Get dressed, Sasha. We can listen on the radio downstairs in the study room. That's where everyone is meeting."

Keenan threw Sasha a rumpled shirt. Suddenly, Sasha sensed the urgency as he grabbed his shoes. "I can put these on downstairs," he said.

Most of the boys in the dorm were gathered in the large study room. The radio was tuned in to the news station. An announcer was broadcasting casualty numbers.

"One thousand men are believed to have died on the **Arizona** alone . . ." said the announcer. There was a quick gasp. Sasha glanced over at a senior named Ted.

"My brother," cried Ted, suddenly ghost white. "My brother was assigned to the Arizona."

"More bombs," whispered Sasha. He thought about his family in Latvia.

The announcer continued, "And now, the President of the United States."

The radio crackled with static. Sasha realized he was holding his breath. The room listened in silence.

Yesterday, December 7, 1941—a date which will live in infamy—the United States of America was suddenly and deliberately attacked by naval and air forces of the empire of Japan.

The United States was at peace with that nation . . .

There is no blinking at the fact that our people, our territory, and our interests are in grave danger.

With confidence in our armed forces—with the unbounding determination of our people—we will gain the inevitable triumph . . . .

I ask that the Congress declare that since the unprovoked and dastardly attack by Japan on Sunday, December 7, a state of war has existed between the United States and the Japanese Empire.

"Turn it off," said Sasha.

"There might be more," protested another boy.

"No," agreed Keenan. He flipped off the dial on the radio. "We've heard enough."

"Go to the master's office, Ted," said Sasha. "Your parents will need you."

"I'll go with you," offered Ralph.

"Don't give up hope, Ted," said Keenan.

Sasha walked over and stared out the window. Snow from the night before had left a thick white blanket. The tracks of two squirrels out searching for an early bite were the only footsteps to mar its surface. Sasha watched their play.

Keenan joined Sasha. He said, "I'm going to join the army."

"What?" said Sasha as he turned. "What about school? You'll graduate in another year."

"I don't think this can wait," said Keenan quietly as he left the room.

5

A Seat on the Train

Sasha lugged his suitcase up the steps. He rushed into the hall of the old train station. For a moment he thought back to another train station. His mother had once hurried him onto a train. He shook himself from the moment of loneliness. Now Moscow seemed so far away.

He smiled and waved as he spotted Keenan standing in the long ticket line.

"Sorry, I'm late," apologized Sasha.

"Looks like everyone wants to go on the same train!" shouted Keenan over the noise.

An announcement echoed. "Express train to New York is now loading on track three."

Impatiently, Sasha waited in the long line to purchase his ticket. Finally they were headed down the dingy ramp to the tracks. They hurried to jump onto the train.

The conductor waved. His piercing whistle signaled their departure. "All aboard!"

Keenan and Sasha moved down the narrow hall. They checked each compartment for two open seats. Each little room was filled. Finally they found an empty seat in the third car.

"You take that one, Keenan," offered Sasha. "I'll go down to the next car. I'll meet you in the dining car in half an hour."

"Right," said Keenan. "I'll look for you when I come down. Hurry, it will be lights out as we leave the station."

Sasha had forgotten about the new blackout rules. The conductor had to make sure no light was showing before the train left the station.

Sasha hurried on, pushing through the double doors between cars. The train had begun to gather speed. The clack of the metal wheels increased in rhythm. The lights were dimmed to small red bulbs in the hallway.

The first two compartments were full. He opened the door to the next darkened compartment. "Excuse me, is there room in here for one more?" he asked.

"Yes, there's one more next to me," replied a quiet voice. She had a heavy Southern accent.

"You're lucky. It might be the last spot on the train," said a second female voice.

"Thanks," said Sasha. He felt in the dark for the luggage rack. He placed his bag among the other packages on the shelf overhead. Then he carefully found the empty spot.

It was totally dark in the compartment. Sasha waited for his eyes to adjust. Even after several minutes, he could see only a few shadows. The windows were heavily masked in thick black cloth. It was a requirement since the beginning of the war.

Sasha sighed and tried to relax. "Uh, hello," he said in a hush. "My name is Sasha."

"My name is Vida," replied the quiet voice. "Across there is my cousin Maryanne."

Maryanne responded with, "Hey."

The soft voice explained. "She's from North Carolina. They say 'hey' for 'hello.' "

Maryanne drawled, "There's someone next to me, but he already went to sleep. Are you getting off at New York?"

"Yes," replied Sasha. "I'm traveling with my friend. We couldn't find seats together. We plan to meet later."

"Where are you from?" asked Vida.

"Well, I go to Yale University now," said Sasha. "But I come from a country in Eastern Europe—Latvia. You probably don't know where that is."

"It's near Russia, isn't it? On the Baltic?" asked Vida. "I've been studying maps lately. More than I used to in geography class."

"Vida has a beau in Europe right now," explained Maryanne.

"A beau?" asked Sasha.

"You know, a boyfriend," said Maryanne.

"Oh," replied Sasha. He didn't know why he was sorry to hear that.

"He's a flier," chatted Maryanne. "He's only been there a couple of months, right, Vida?"

"Four months and five days," sighed Vida.

"She's been so heartsick. I told her she had to get out and do something. It isn't right to sit around and sulk," drawled Maryanne.

"Maryanne, he doesn't care," said Vida.

"I'm sorry," Vida apologized to Sasha.

"Do you work or go to school?" asked Sasha, trying to change the subject. He wanted to hear Vida's soft, low voice again.

"I'm in school," said Vida. "Working on my degree.

Do you think it's silly for a woman to want an education?"

"No," said Sasha. "And where is your uh . . . beau?" He'd ask anything to hear her voice.

"England. He signed up almost a year ago. He was going to be in the RAF, the English Air Force. But that's all changed because of Pearl Harbor. His last letter said that they would be in an American unit. I think he will fly a bomber, but he can't say," Vida explained.

"Everything has to be a big secret," said Maryanne.

"He felt it was important to go," Vida added.

Sasha could hear Maryanne searching through her bag. "Ah-ha. There you are. Vida, honey, I'm going to go down to the ladies room for a bit to touch up my lipstick. Do you want to come?"

"No, thanks," said Vida. Sasha's heart gave a little leap.

"Now you be a gentleman," Maryanne ordered Sasha.

"Yes, ma'am," mocked Sasha.

Vida giggled.

"See y'all later," Maryanne called. She closed the compartment door. The gentleman in the fourth seat snored once. Then he moaned and was quiet.

"She's really very sweet," Vida defended Maryanne. "She's five years older than I am. She mothers me something awful. I know the drawl is a little thick."

"We all have our accents. I can't complain," laughed Sasha.

"I like yours. It's very romantic," said Vida.

Sasha smiled. "Thanks," he said. He was glad it was dark. Vida couldn't see him blush.

"Sasha is an interesting name," continued Vida.

His heart took another little skip.

"Well, it's really a nickname," explained Sasha. "My real name is Alexander Victorovich Bausch." He said this in a deep, important tone.

Vida smiled in the dark. "Yes, Sasha is easier."

"Actually, I changed my last name to Baxter when I moved to the United States," he explained. "I'll become a citizen as soon as I'm allowed. I loved Latvia, but America seems like home."

"How long have you been in the United States?"

"Since 1939. I came before the war in Europe started," said Sasha.

"Now I guess we call it World War II," said Vida.

"And do you still have family, uh, over there?" asked Vida.

"Yes," whispered Sasha. He couldn't bear to talk about his family. "Tell me about your family," he continued, changing the subject again.

Vida understood. She knew what it was like to miss someone far away.

"My family is in Illinois," she told him. "I came out to Boston for school."

A Seat on the Train

There was a loud knock at the compartment door. Sasha heard Keenan calling his name. "You there, Sasha?"

"I'm here," replied Sasha.

Keenan opened the door. "I have a reservation for us in the dining car. The porter said we could slip in right now. Come on, I'm starving," ordered Keenan.

"Would you like to join us?" Sasha asked Vida.

"No, I need to wait for Maryanne," said Vida.

Sasha was disappointed.

"Come on, Sasha," said Keenan impatiently.

"See you later," Vida said.

"I'd like that," replied Sasha.

"Sasha," asked Vida as he stood in the doorway. "What's your favorite American food?"

Sasha paused. He looked back into the glow of the red emergency hall light. He could almost see the shape of her face and the wave of soft blond hair.

"Cherry sodas," he responded. He left to find Keenan.

The boys entered the dining car. Sasha could see a few low lights on the table.

"That's better," said Keenan. "I was wondering how we would eat in the dark."

"I rather liked the dark," said Sasha.

Sasha and Keenan waited in the crowded dining car. Over the racket, Sasha heard Bing Crosby singing

"White Christmas" on the radio. They were finally seated.

A frazzled waiter came to take their order. "Sorry," he said. "I still can't get used to the low lighting. And there are so many people traveling these days. Everyone needs to get somewhere else now that there is war."

Sasha began to speak. The waiter suddenly froze. He stared at Sasha.

"Wait a minute. You aren't one of those Germans, are you?" he asked.

"He is not a German," Keenan said defensively.

"Are you sure?" accused the waiter. He eyed Sasha suspiciously. "You sound funny."

"I am Russian. I came from Latvia to go to school," explained Sasha.

"We're supposed to keep an eye out for Nazis now, you know," continued the waiter.

Sasha could tell that Keenan was getting angry.

"Hey, man!" shouted Keenan. "His family's been bombed by the Nazis too! He doesn't even know if they're still alive."

"Sorry," apologized the waiter. "No offense."

"It's alright," said Sasha. He stared hard at his menu.

They quickly ordered their sandwiches. The waiter disappeared.

"People are so strange now," said Keenan.

40

A Seat on the Train

Sasha stared into the little candle on the table.

"I'm . . . I'm sure they're alright. Your family, I mean . . ." continued Keenan. "Sorry, Sasha. I didn't mean to upset you. We're supposed to be having a little vacation. Come on. It's Christmas."

"If only another letter from Raisa would come," sighed Sasha. "And I've only had one letter from my mother since she was released from prison. She's getting older now. Mama always had to work so hard."

Keenan tried to change the subject. "Who were you talking to back there?" he asked. "She sounded very pretty."

"She has a beautiful voice," agreed Sasha. "I never did get a good look at her. Her name is Vida."

"Did you find out where she's from?" asked Keenan.

"Just Boston," said Sasha.

"Last name? School?" asked Keenan.

"No. I'm hopeless," moaned Sasha.

"Never mind," laughed Keenan.

Their sandwiches arrived. The waiter didn't look at Sasha as he put them on the table.

"Let's eat quickly and go back," suggested Sasha.

Keenan nodded.

After dinner, Sasha led the way back to the compartment. He opened the door and called, "Vida?"

No one answered.

"Maryanne?"

A gentle snore replied.

"They'll probably be back soon. We can wait for them here," suggested Keenan.

Sasha felt for his suitcase and then noticed that it was alone on the shelf.

"Oh, no," he groaned. "She took her things."

"She might come back," said Keenan hopefully.

Sasha wasn't so sure. "I might never see her again."

"You never did see her," reminded Keenan.

Now that the girls had left, Sasha and Keenan were able to sit together for the rest of the trip.

Sasha could tell when the train was approaching New York City. The sound the wheels made changed as it slowed and crossed a long bridge. Usually Sasha could see the lights of the skyscrapers. Now the blackout curtains limited his view.

"That was probably the bridge over the East River," said Keenan. "We made good time."

"Let's get off quickly," said Sasha. "I want to see if I can find Vida in the crowd."

Keenan shook his head. "You've got it bad," he joked.

Sasha was waiting to hop off the train as soon as it slowed. He hurried down the ramp next to the tracks. He almost ran up the steps to the platform.

From this view, he scanned the crowd. He searched for Vida's face but then realized that he didn't know her face. He saw two girls walking together and approached.

"Vida?" he asked hopefully.

The girls stared at him for a moment. Then they giggled and hurried away.

Keenan caught up with Sasha. "You'll never find her in this mob," he said.

Sasha scanned the last stragglers. Then he gave up.

"I guess I look pretty silly," sighed Sasha. He picked up his suitcase and tried to smile.

"Never mind, friend," comforted Keenan. "There are plenty more girls out there. Wait until we go to the club tonight. Let's catch a taxi and get to my folks' house."

They bundled into the back of a neon yellow taxicab.

"Brooklyn," instructed Keenan.

Sasha began to relax. Their driver wove his way through the evening traffic. It would be good not to think about homework, classes, and work for a few days.

Sasha let out a big sigh. Keenan studied his face.

"Ground rules," said Keenan. He shook his finger playfully at Sasha. "You are not to say anything to my parents about my plan to enlist."

Sasha started to shake his head.

Keenan was very serious. "I mean it, Sasha. You can't upset them. It won't do any good. I've already signed on."

"You have!" exclaimed Sasha. "You didn't tell me

that. When?"

"I just did it today. I wasn't even sure until I had the pen in my hand. But listen, Sasha. I don't go until after term. The Army Air Corps isn't ready to train me yet. And it will take almost a year to go through the training. I have a million things to learn."

Sasha could see how excited Keenan was.

"I'm going to learn how to fly!" Keenan shouted. The taxi driver looked over his shoulder in surprise. He grinned at them in the rearview mirror.

"And besides, this old war will probably be over by the time I'm ready," said Keenan.

"I don't know about that," doubted Sasha.

"Now that we Americans are in it, we'll have Hitler on the run in no time," agreed the driver.

Sasha thought back to his time in Riga. He remembered when the Nazis had marched around the Freedom Monument. How could he explain the evil in the Nazis' eyes to Keenan? Sasha doubted Hitler would be so easy to defeat.

"Sasha?" Keenan was suddenly serious. "Will you go?"

Sasha studied the darkened high-rises out the taxi's window.

"I don't know," he said.

6

Uncle Jesse

Keenan paid the cab driver as Sasha unloaded their bags. They hurried up the steps of the townhouse. Keenan's mother opened the front door as they reached the top step.

"Hi, Ma," called Keenan.

"Come here, you," Mrs. Murphy playfully ordered. "Give your ma a big hug. I see you brought Sasha."

"Hello, Mrs. Murphy," said Sasha. "Thanks for inviting me."

Mrs. Murphy smiled. "I told Keenan that if he didn't bring you this time, he wasn't to come home."

Keenan laughed. "Told you, didn't I?"

Mrs. Murphy gave Sasha a motherly hug.

"Oh, Sasha, you're too thin," she said. "Keenan, go in the kitchen and get this boy a banana."

"I'm fine, really," insisted Sasha. "We ate on the train."

"Never mind. We'll get you fattened up over Christmas. Don't they feed you well at school?" she asked.

"We brought our laundry, Ma," said Keenan. He dropped two large white duffels onto the floor.

"Of course," said Mrs. Murphy with a small grimace. "Go on in the living room. Your Uncle Jesse is here too. He came down from Buffalo yesterday."

"Uncle Jesse's here!" exclaimed Keenan. "Great! I didn't know he was coming. Come on, Sasha."

Sasha already knew Uncle Jesse from other visits. He was glad to see him again.

Uncle Jesse rolled his wheelchair forward as the boys entered the room. Keenan quickly dropped to one knee. They gave each other a welcoming hug.

"I'm so glad to see you, Uncle Jesse," said Keenan.

Sasha offered his hand. He was greeted with a beaming smile and gripping handshake.

"Good to see you, sir," said Sasha.

"Ah, Alexander Victorovich." Uncle Jesse's blue eyes twinkled. "I hear you have learned my famous rear attack."

"Yes, sir. It's come in handy too," responded Sasha.

Keenan said, "Sasha won the last foil tournament with that move. He's getting really good. Sasha and I will both compete in **epee**. That way Yale can do even better in the regional competition."

"I've thought of a new counter for you, Keenan," said Uncle Jesse. "We can work on it later. What are you boys doing tonight?"

"We're meeting Ralph at Nick's later," said Keenan. "There's a good jazz group there on Friday nights. Would you like to come?"

"Yes," encouraged Sasha.

"You boys don't need an old man slowing you down," argued Uncle Jesse.

"We insist," said Sasha.

Uncle Jesse grinned.

The boys enjoyed dinner with the family. They shared stories of the past few weeks. Everyone was concerned about the war, but the spirit of Christmas kept them from lingering on the topic.

It was past midnight when they finally arrived at Nick's in Greenwich Village. It was impossible for Uncle Jesse to negotiate the steps down to the basement club. Finally Keenan and Sasha just picked him up, chair and all, and hauled him down.

"Thanks, boys," said Uncle Jesse. They settled themselves at one of the tiny round tables. "I try not to let these legs of mine slow me down, but steps . . ."

"Not a problem," insisted Sasha. "Besides, we'll have Ralph to help us back up."

Ralph was making his way to their table now.

"Hello, everyone," greeted Ralph.

"How was the drive down?" asked Keenan.

"Fine, no snow yet," said Ralph. "My mother ordered a chair for my grandmother at Gimbals Department Store," he explained. "I had to drive down and be the delivery boy."

"You make a good Santa Claus," joked Keenan. Sasha groaned, but Ralph grinned good-naturedly.

"Good thing the gas rationing hasn't started yet," said Uncle Jesse.

Ralph pulled up a chair. The little band struck up. For a while, they just listened to the mellow jazz.

"So how are the puzzles for Professor Casey coming along?" asked Ralph during a break in the music.

Sasha shrugged. "I was really struggling over one equation last week. But usually they're just rather long and tedious."

"What are the equations for?" asked Uncle Jesse.

Keenan said, "Sasha doesn't know. He just does these huge equations. Then he adds them to a graph. Has the professor ever explained?" he asked Sasha.

Sasha shook his head and shrugged. "No, but the equations seem to fit a pattern."

Uncle Jesse was curious. "The answers or the equations?"

"The equations," Sasha responded. "And there are letters that fit in too. I did a graph last week that had more letters than numbers."

"Does Professor Casey work for the government?" asked Uncle Jesse.

Ralph asked, "Do you think he's a spy?" His blue eyes grew wide in his round face.

Uncle Jesse shrugged. "He could be doing some **encryption** work."

"Wow," said Keenan. "Do you think so?"

Sasha was concerned. "I hadn't thought of that. But for who?"

It was a question that worried Sasha the rest of the night.

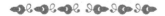

Sasha woke up early. He rekindled the fire in the parlor. The rest of the house was fast asleep.

Early winter light shone through the bare branches of the trees. Leftover snow from an earlier fall formed patches on the sidewalk. Sasha watched a few hardy sparrows fluff their feathers to protect themselves from the cold.

Uncle Jesse quietly rolled into the room.

"Well, another early bird," he said.

"Good morning," said Sasha. "I made coffee if you want some."

"Thank you," said Uncle Jesse.

Sasha returned from the kitchen with a steaming cup. Uncle Jesse had rolled his chair close to the window. Sasha sat beside him.

Uncle Jesse blew on and then sipped the hot brew. His blue eyes crinkled in the corners. Gray hair, a little long, was neatly brushed off his thin face. Sasha was reminded of Lazare, a long-ago friend from Moscow.

"Keenan is joining up, isn't he?" asked Uncle Jesse.

Sasha was caught by surprise. He was unsure how to respond. He tried to look away. He didn't want to lie.

Uncle Jesse smiled. "No, he hasn't told me. But I know that boy very well. He'll think he must serve. He thinks it's his duty. Am I right?"

Sasha shook his head in agreement. "He wants to fly. He just doesn't know what . . ." Sasha didn't know how to put his fear into words.

"What he's letting himself in for?" Uncle Jesse

completed the sentence. "I have a feeling that you know," he continued. "Keenan has told me a little. I know you were smuggled out of Moscow as a boy. I know your mother was punished for that."

"A year in a gulag," whispered Sasha. "I have seen what prison can do to people. I have seen so much fear and desperation."

"And you again had to flee before the war in Europe heated up," Uncle Jesse said.

"My sister knew how dangerous it would become for me. She and others wanted me to go. Now I know they were right," said Sasha.

"And where is your family now?" asked Uncle Jesse.

"My entire family is trapped in the war." Sasha looked away. "Maybe worse." He willed his eyes not to tear. He clenched his hands into fists.

"I don't know anything. I may never know. And I'm not the only one," said Sasha.

"There is evil in the war. We must be careful," said Uncle Jesse.

"Someone else said that to me once," sighed Sasha, thinking again of Lazare.

"You understand far more of what this world is facing than most Americans. Young men like Keenan only see the glory," Uncle Jesse said.

"Or honor," added Sasha.

"There's no such thing as an honorable war," stated Uncle Jesse firmly.

"But we can't stand by and do nothing!" exclaimed Sasha. "I'm not afraid to go, though I probably should be. I just don't know how to best serve. My family has sent me so far. They have given up so much for me. Would it be fair for me to turn around and die on some battlefield?"

Uncle Jesse stared out the window for a long moment.

"Each of us finds a way," he finally said. "Just make certain that it really counts."

"You gave in the last war," Sasha pointed out. "Keenan told me that you were wounded. That was how . . ."

Uncle Jesse shook his head sadly. "Did he tell you how this happened?" The man patted his lifeless legs.

"No," replied Sasha. "Keenan just said you were injured in World War I. He's so proud of you. You have a Purple Heart."

"I was run over by a tank," said the man bitterly. "One of ours. There is no pride in that."

7

Suspicion

Sasha's chemistry class was finally over. He hurried
down the darkened street toward the math building.
The snow was deep on the lawns, but it packed down
underfoot. Sasha's boots squeaked as he hurried along.

Twilight came very early now, before 5:00. Sasha buried his nose in his scarf. He sprinted the rest of the way.

He stopped on the steps of the math building to stamp the snow from his boots. Dim light from a nearby window reflected on the snow. Sasha recognized Professor Casey quietly talking to a man dressed in a long overcoat and **homburg** hat.

The professor handed the man a large brown envelope. The man slipped it into his coat. Then he melted into the darkness.

Professor Casey glanced around. Then he hurried off in the opposite direction.

Sasha entered the building. What was Professor Casey doing out in the dark? Who was that man with him? The man in the homburg didn't look familiar. Sasha couldn't shake the strange feeling he had.

Sasha unlocked Professor Casey's office. He had a key because he often worked when the professor was out. Sasha turned on the light and shed his coat. He glanced over at the professor's messy desk.

"You couldn't find anything in there, even if you wanted to," chuckled Sasha to himself.

He noticed a small crumpled note in an otherwise empty garbage can. Sasha's curiosity caught hold. He picked up the slip of paper and smoothed it. "Rottweiler, 4:45" was all that was written on it.

Sasha stared out the window for a moment. "It doesn't mean anything," he said to himself. Yet he slipped the note into his pocket.

Sasha sat down at the small table in the corner. Professor Casey had left him a new set of formulas. He looked around for the graph he had completed yesterday. He couldn't find it.

Sasha got up and carefully searched the professor's desk. He checked the file where he kept his work. He checked the bookcase. His work was gone.

A key jiggled in the lock. Guiltily, Sasha hurried back to his desk. Professor Casey walked in, carelessly tossing his hat on the chair. The professor jumped when he noticed Sasha.

"Oh, Mr. Baxter. You're here late. I didn't expect you today."

"Yes, sir. I had chemistry class today. I needed to check a few equations on my graph. I can't find it though," said Sasha.

"Uh, yes. I checked it over last night." The professor's eyes darted away. "Everything was fine. In fact, you did an excellent job. You finished that one very quickly."

"Thank you," said Sasha.

Suddenly, Professor Casey seemed in a hurry to leave. He brushed a nervous hand through his trim white beard.

"I sent, I mean, I *have* it," stumbled the professor. His fingers fidgeted with his lapels.

"You never have told me what the graphs are for," stated Sasha.

"No? Well, don't worry about that. You're doing a fine job. I have to go now. My wife is waiting. G—goodnight, Sasha," the man stammered.

Professor Casey rushed out quickly. He had forgotten his hat.

Sasha watched the professor dash from the building into the cold darkness. It was beginning to snow again.

8

Vida

Sasha sat at the counter of the tiny drugstore. The soda jerk in a white paper hat placed a cherry soda before him. Sasha stirred the sweet drink. The melting ice cream streamed into the pink liquid.

"Could I have one too?" asked a quiet voice behind him.

"*Vida?*" Sasha turned. He couldn't help grinning. "What are you doing here?" he asked.

Vida smiled briefly. She slid in next to him on a low swivel stool. She pushed a short blond curl off her forehead.

"It wasn't that hard to find you." She suddenly blushed. "You must think I'm very forward."

"No, no. I would have gone looking for you, but I never got your last name. I didn't even know where you went to school. I came back to ask you on the train. But you were already gone. I . . ." Sasha stopped. His ears turned bright red.

Vida smiled. But Sasha thought that her eyes looked sad.

"I came on the train this morning. I needed someone to talk to," Vida explained. "I knew you went to Yale. I just asked around."

The man behind the counter brought her a tall pink glass. Ice cream dripped down the side.

"What's the matter?" asked Sasha. He didn't know how he knew. But he could sense something was wrong.

She stared at the soda. A tear rolled down her cheek.

"It's Don." She took a hesitant breath. "I heard from his parents. His plane went down over Holland."

Sasha took her hand. "I'm so sorry."

"He died and I didn't even know," she cried. "I was sleeping in my safe warm bed and he just . . . died." Sasha handed her his handkerchief.

"Oh, Vida . . ." whispered Sasha.

She wiped her tears away. "I didn't have anyone to talk to. My roommate is out of town. Maryanne is in Atlanta. My family is far away. There's no one else at school . . ."

"I'm so glad you found me," said Sasha. He was still holding her hand.

Sasha and Vida strolled through campus. The New Haven Green was covered with deep snow, but the sidewalks were cleared. Bright winter sun reflected off the silvery snow. It shot long shadows off the sleeping elm trees.

"When I read the letter the first time, I didn't even understand the words. It couldn't be about my Don. I was sure there had been a mistake," explained Vida.

"You just didn't want it to be true," said Sasha.

"But then it hit me. I realized what it meant. I would never see him again. I was so scared. My heart was pounding. I couldn't catch my breath. The room was spinning." Sasha just nodded and kept listening.

"I just sat down and stared out the window," Vida continued. "I remember it was almost dark. I don't remember much about the rest of the night. I don't even know if I slept." Vida paused.

"When it was light, I knew I had to come find you," she continued. She shook her head. "Is that crazy?"

"No," said Sasha. "I'm glad you did."

"But I'd never even seen your face," said Vida.

"Probably better that way. I have big ears." He wiggled them for her.

Vida couldn't help smiling. "Yes, you do. But you have kind eyes. I guess I knew you could be a friend by your voice."

"I think it was a great way to meet," said Sasha.

"I must get back to the train station," sighed Vida. "The last train for Boston leaves at five."

"I'll come with you," said Sasha.

It was only a short walk to the station. When they arrived, Vida checked the track number. She pulled her return ticket from her purse. The sleek train hissed on the track next to them.

They stood together at the steps. Vida turned to face Sasha.

"I have a little time," she said.

"I don't like train stations very much," said Sasha, looking around.

"Why?" asked Vida.

"I don't like saying good-bye. Although, I'm usually the one leaving," said Sasha.

"Your family?" asked Vida.

"Yes." He hesitated for a moment. "My family is . . . Actually, I don't know . . ."

"I didn't mean to pry," she said.

"No, it's okay. My mother lives in Moscow," he explained.

"Oh dear. Things are so awful there this winter. I'm so sorry. Do you have other family?" she asked.

"Yes, in Riga. It's not much better there." Sasha felt better now that she knew.

"It's been a long time since I've heard from them," he said. "They could be fine. It's just not knowing that's hard. I can't read the war reports in the paper. They seem so . . ."

"Distant? Unreal?" Vida finished the sentence.

"Yes. I guess I see the war in very personal terms," concluded Sasha. "I read about starving children, and I wonder about my little nephew. I hear about bombs falling and think about my mother and sister. I have known Nazis. They are to be feared. It is hard for most Americans to understand this."

Vida shivered.

"I'm sorry. I don't want to upset you more," apologized Sasha.

"No," said Vida. "That's why it's a world war. No one escapes the suffering."

She put her arms around his waist and laid her head on his chest. He kissed her hair and hugged her twice.

"One for now and one for later," whispered Vida. "That's what my mother always says."

Sasha gasped. His mother had said the same thing to him as a child.

The conductor blew his whistle.

Startled, Vida turned and jumped up the two steps onto the train. The train crept forward.

In a panic, Sasha cried, "I still don't know your last name. I don't have your address."

"I'll write you when I get home," Vida called out. "Thank you, Sasha."

He had started to run alongside the train as it left the station. The noise from the engine was deafening. The wheels clattered on the tracks as they gathered speed.

"You promise?" yelled Sasha.

"What?" cried Vida over the roar.

"Promise?" shouted Sasha. He stood at the end of the ramp.

"Yes," she called and blew him a kiss.

Sasha wandered into dinner very late.

"Where have you been?" asked Ralph. "I don't think you made it in time for dinner."

"I don't care," sighed Sasha. He collapsed into a chair. Grinning, he rested his chin in his hands.

"Since when did the eating machine not want dinner?" laughed Keenan.

"What's wrong with him?" asked Ralph. He studied Sasha's face. "He looks really dopey."

Sasha smiled. "Keenan, do you remember the girl on the train?"

Keenan smiled. "The one whose face you never saw?"

Sasha nodded.

"The one whose number you forgot to get?" continued Keenan.

Sasha nodded.

"The one you have been mooning over for weeks?" asked Ralph.

"I don't moon," objected Sasha.

"Sure," laughed Keenan.

"I just sometimes dreamed about seeing her again," explained Sasha.

"Well?" asked Ralph and Keenan.

"She came and found me!" announced Sasha.

Keenan hooted and Ralph cheered.

"What's her name?" Ralph asked.

"Vida," sighed Sasha.

"You already knew that," said Keenan. "Did you get her number? Where does she go to school?"

"I don't know." Sasha shrugged.

The friends groaned loudly.

"But she said she'd write," said Sasha. And somehow, he was sure she would.

February 23, 1942

Dear Sasha,

I will never be able to thank you enough for helping me when I came to find you. I was so upset. Now I feel that I am climbing out of the darkness.

I've quit school. It doesn't seem important now. I found a job in an engineering office. They manufacture parts for fighters. To my surprise (and that of the men in the office), I am very good at reading blueprints and figuring formulas. They are training me to help build airplanes. I've been working 18 hours a day for weeks.

I moved out of the school dorm. I'm living with several other girls from the factory. We have a wonderful time together. Maryanne has come to stay for a while. She says she wants to get a job too.

Next week I have my first Saturday off. Will you come to visit?

I'm sorry it took so long to write. You've been in my thoughts.

Vida

P.S. The early train arrives at 10:30. My address is 143 Prince Street, Boston. It's just a block from the train station.

"Tell me about Poppy," said Vida. They were sitting at the soda fountain. Sasha sucked the last of his cherry soda noisily.

He considered the question and said, "Think of a sweet old babushka."

"English please. What is a babushka?" laughed Vida.

"Uh . . . grandmother. Officially she was my nanny, but she was really more like a grandmother. She always smelled like cinnamon. That's Poppy," said Sasha.

"Do you miss her?" asked Vida.

Sasha smiled sadly. "I miss her twice as much now."

Vida looked puzzled.

"I had to leave her behind two times. The first time was in Moscow. Then, years later, she was allowed to come to us in Latvia. Then I left again."

"She'll be okay," Vida assured him.

"Yes, she will," agreed Sasha. "She's probably taking care of everyone and doing it better than anyone could."

"When did you decide you wanted to come to the United States?" asked Vida.

"I didn't want to," said Sasha.

"No?" Vida's voice sounded surprised.

"No, I wanted to stay with my family. My father died, and my sister and her family were all I had. It was my sister, Raisa, who insisted I leave." Sasha shook his head. "I was very stubborn."

"What changed your mind?" asked Vida.

"I saw the evils of war," answered Sasha honestly. "I had a friend. I thought I knew him. He and Ralph and I were great friends. We did everything together."

"Like the Three Musketeers?" suggested Vida.

Sasha grimaced. "His name was Dieter. I found out he was a Nazi."

Vida shivered.

"He was the one who convinced me to leave. I would have stayed and ignored all the warnings. But Dieter helped me to see what the Nazis could do to someone I loved. That's when I understood that I had to escape before it was too late," said Sasha.

"Then, somehow, he was *still* your friend," Vida pointed out.

9

Parry

Sasha had finished his homework except for English. He sighed as he flipped through the pages of *Hamlet* he had to read by tomorrow. He picked up the book and settled into the one comfortable chair in the dorm room.

Suddenly, Keenan and Ralph returned from a midnight raid on the kitchen.

"What did you find?" asked Sasha. His stomach rumbled.

"I found fixings for sandwiches," cheered Keenan.

Ralph followed him into the room. "I found the cookies that the cook had hidden for tomorrow's lunch." Ralph grinned and held up the loot.

"Snickerdoodles?" asked Sasha.

"Yep," agreed Ralph.

"*Hamlet* can wait," said Sasha. He tossed his book on the chair and helped put together their late-night feast.

"Any pickles?" Sasha asked.

Ralph moaned, "Rats. I knew we forgot something."

"Never mind," said Sasha.

"I guess I'll be roughing it when I hit boot camp in two weeks. No more midnight raids for me," Keenan pointed out.

Ralph nodded. "I hear it's awful. You march and march and march some more."

"Seems silly to learn how to march when you're going to be flying," said Sasha.

Keenan nodded with a mouthful. "I'll tell my sergeant that."

Sasha was suddenly serious. "It won't be the same here without you, Keenan."

Ralph agreed.

"Come with me," suggested Keenan.

"Not me," said Ralph. "I get dizzy on the third floor."

"What about you, Sasha?" asked Keenan.

Sasha sighed. "I just got out of Europe. I'm not going back. But I do wish I could do more than sit in a classroom."

"You'll do a lot of good," Keenan told him. "You only have one more year now that they're kicking us all out ahead of time."

"It's great that they need Yale for military training. I think I'm going to go into language translation. The recruiter said—" Ralph blurted. Then he stopped, embarrassed.

"You went down to the recruiter?" asked Sasha. "But you aren't a citizen either."

"I don't even have to join the army," explained Ralph. "I'll be part of the State Department or something like that."

"Maybe *you* could be a spy," suggested Keenan.

Sasha hoped his friend was joking.

"Well, you speak all those languages," Keenan pointed out.

"Maybe you are already working for a spy, Sasha," joshed Ralph.

"You may not be so far from the truth there. I'm really worried about Professor Casey," said Sasha.

"Why?" both boys asked.

"Remember those graphs I was working on? I never told you, but I think I saw Professor Casey hand over the last graph to a very mysterious man."

"What do you mean 'mysterious'?" asked Ralph.

"They met in the dark in front of the math building. Professor Casey handed the man an envelope," explained Sasha. "It gave me the creeps."

"When did you see this?" asked Keenan.

"A couple of weeks ago," said Sasha. "I forgot about it."

Ralph nudged Keenan. "He's been thinking about the little blond."

"I tried to ask the professor about it," continued Sasha. "He acted like a scared rabbit. Oh, I found this note too."

Sasha showed them the slip of paper he had found.

"Rottweiler could be a German name," said Ralph.

"Hmm," said Keenan thoughtfully. "Maybe we should set a little trap for this rabbit."

"Yeah," agreed Ralph.

"What would we do?" asked Sasha.

Keenan paced up and down the room for a few moments. He chewed his sandwich thoughtfully. Then his face lit up.

"I know!" he shouted. "My friend Matt lives in Silliman Hall. That's across from the math building. He'd let us keep an eye on Professor Casey."

"I almost have the next graph done," Sasha said. "I only have a few more equations to work through."

"Stall a day or two. We'll begin as soon as we return from the fencing tournament in Boston," instructed Keenan. "Pretend the last problems are more difficult. That will give us time to set this up. We'll have to watch him and get used to his schedule."

"That shouldn't be too hard," said Sasha. "That man does everything by the clock."

10

The Tournament

Sasha searched the crowd. She had promised to come. He knew that his bouts wouldn't begin for an hour. He tried to relax, releasing his breath slowly.

"I've been looking for you," said Vida from behind him. "You're hard to find in that outfit."

"Hi, Vida." He gave her a quick hug.

"Hey," said Maryanne. "I came along to see what this fencing is all about."

"Hey," repeated Sasha.

"Vida, honey, this is great," Maryanne drawled. "Look at all these handsome men. They look like movie stars. I'll just mosey along and see what I can find."

Vida smiled at Sasha.

"Are you nervous?" she asked him.

"A little," admitted Sasha. "I want Yale to rank well."

"You'll do fine," she encouraged.

"Sure he will," agreed Uncle Jesse.

Keenan had rolled his uncle's chair up to meet them.

"Look who I found," said Keenan.

"Well, I had to watch my boys get first place in the tournament," stated Uncle Jesse.

"Uncle Jesse, this is my . . ."

"Girlfriend," finished Vida as she shook his hand. "I'm Vida. I've heard about you, Uncle Jesse."

"Don't believe a word." The old man blushed.

"Come on, Sasha," said Keenan. "The team meeting is starting in a minute."

"Good luck," called Vida. Sasha waved as Keenan dragged him away.

After the meeting, the boys warmed up together. Then the bouts began.

Keenan won his first round easily. Sasha, too, had taken his first-round bouts. The second round worried him.

Through the luck of the draw, Sasha was facing the captain of the Harvard team. The tournament would go to either Harvard or Yale. Princeton had already fallen far behind in total points. Sasha knew his team needed him to continue into the final round.

Keenan whistled as he saw who Sasha would face next.

Sasha stepped onto the strip. The epee felt good in his hand. He knew that he could score anywhere on his opponent, not just on the torso as with the foil.

Sasha glanced over to the crowd. Uncle Jesse gave him a victory sign. Vida just smiled.

His opponent was fast and smart. He had two touches on Sasha in a few moments—one on Sasha's mask, another on his knee. This was tough.

"Settle down, Sasha," he told himself.

Sasha battled back. He won two points with a steady rhythm.

Again they matched points.

"Three to three!" shouted the director.

Each battled hard for the fourth point. His opponent struggled for breath as Sasha grabbed the fourth point.

His opponent roared right back with a hard jab to Sasha's ribs.

"Match point," called the director. "On guard."

Blades touched. Once, twice, three times, Sasha initiated an attack. Then he parried and backed away.

Sasha thought he could see a smile on his opponent's face through the mask. Sasha kept his face serious.

Again Sasha attacked, but this time he fletched instead of retreating. He made a lightning-fast touch to his opponent's mask. His blade made a perfect arch but flexed so quickly that none of the judges saw the point.

Then the tip of his blade broke. It sprung into the air and clattered as it hit the floor. No one but Sasha saw. No one heard it either.

His opponent parried, and Sasha saw an opening. There's no time, he thought to himself. Sasha stepped out of the strip and took the point against him. He wouldn't risk injuring his opponent with an unguarded blade.

"Match to Harvard, five to four," called the director.

Sasha's opponent picked up the broken tip. He walked forward and shook Sasha's hand.

"You're a great fencer," he stated.

It had to be enough, thought Sasha.

"Sorry," said Sasha as he rejoined his team.

"Don't worry," said Keenan. "We can still get them."

Uncle Jesse nodded, still smiling.

Keenan was in the final round. Sasha sat with Uncle Jesse, Vida, and Maryanne.

"Go, Keenan!" shouted the girls.

"He really is good," said Uncle Jesse as he watched his nephew take the third touch. "When does he leave for the army?"

"Next week," said Sasha.

Keenan's epee slashed the air. His footwork was flawless.

Uncle Jesse sighed.

"Don't worry," Sasha assured Uncle Jesse. "He'll fly jets just like he fences."

"Bout to Yale, five to two. Tournament to Yale," the loud speaker echoed.

11

Catching a Spy

"How long has Professor Casey been in his office?" asked Sasha. He and Ralph had just returned to their lookout.

"All through dinner," moaned Keenan. "I'm starving."

"Here, we brought you some rolls and chicken," offered Ralph.

"Thanks," said Keenan. He attacked the chicken leg.

Ralph took up Keenan's place by the window.

"This spy business is boring," complained Ralph. "We've been watching the professor for three days. Nothing has happened."

"I'll do the late shift tonight if you have homework," offered Sasha.

"Did you finish the last of the equations?" asked Keenan.

Sasha nodded.

"I gave the graph to him yesterday afternoon," he said. "Then I left. I thought he might make the call right away."

"Good thinking," said Keenan. "We know Professor Casey usually works until 6:30. It's almost 7:00 now. He's still there, so this could be the night."

"What do we do if we see this guy?" asked Ralph. A worried look crossed his brow.

"We could follow him," suggested Sasha.

"No. If we see them meeting, we'll sneak down. Then we'll try to grab the guy," argued Keenan.

Sasha looked doubtful.

"What if he has a gun?" asked Ralph.

Keenan rolled his eyes.

"Well, if he is a spy, he could have a gun," insisted Ralph.

"Ralph is right," agreed Sasha. "We should be careful. Maybe we should follow him to a public place. Then we could challenge him."

"Following him could be difficult," said Keenan. "Especially in the dark."

The other two looked worried.

"Okay, okay, we'll follow him," he agreed reluctantly.

The evening dragged on. The single light in Professor Casey's window glowed in the dark building.

Ralph looked back from the slit in the curtains. "This is so boring," he sighed.

"I'll watch for a while," offered Sasha.

"Wait," Ralph whispered, glancing back at the window. "His light just went out."

"You don't need to whisper," Keenan pointed out. "He can't hear you."

Sasha peeked out. "Look! There by the tree. A man is standing in the shadow just off the path," he whispered.

"Turn out the light," suggested Keenan. "Then we can all watch out the window. They won't be able to see us."

Sasha hit the switch. Pale moonlight lit the faces of the three boys. They huddled in the narrow space in front of the window.

Professor Casey opened the front door of the math building and walked down the steps. The mysterious man in a homburg hat stepped forward to greet him.

"Come on!" exclaimed Sasha. "That's the same man."

"We're right behind you," said Keenan.

The boys bolted down the steps three at a time. They stopped just inside the main archway of the college. Everyone yanked on heavy jackets. Sasha pulled a hat down to cover his face. They could still see the two men across the road.

"Quietly now. We don't want to spook them," hissed Keenan.

Sasha and Ralph nodded quickly.

"I brought a football," said Ralph.

"What?" asked Keenan, confused.

"We can pretend to play a little catch. They won't think we're paying any attention to them," explained Ralph.

Sasha smiled. "Good thinking, Ralph."

Lampposts dimly lit the night. Deep snow lay drifted beside the sidewalks. The boys walked across the empty road. They tossed the football back and forth.

The closer they came to their suspects, the faster Sasha's heart beat. He kept his back to Professor Casey. Sasha hoped the man wouldn't recognize him.

Sasha glanced toward the men. He saw Professor

Casey hand over a large envelope to the man in the homburg. The man turned and walked away quickly.

Suddenly Keenan took off. He sprinted the last 50 yards as the man disappeared into the shadows. Sasha raced to catch up. Ahead, Sasha heard a shout and a thud.

"Keenan, are you okay? We were only going to follow him, remember?" yelled Sasha. He prayed Ralph was wrong about the gun.

Ralph quickly caught up to them. Keenan had tackled the man. They both lay on the frozen ground.

"Get off me!" shouted the man. "What do you think you're doing?"

Professor Casey ran up. "Sasha, what on earth is going on here? What is Keenan doing?"

"I'm catching a spy," announced Keenan proudly. He pulled the man to his feet. Ralph and Keenan grabbed the man's arms.

"We know he has the work that Sasha does. It's a code, isn't it? Are you a German spy?" Ralph asked the man.

"No, no," said the professor. "You have it all wrong, Sasha."

The man brushed himself off. He began to smile.

"So this is Sasha," he said. "I think that perhaps we should explain a few things."

"Let's go into my office," suggested Professor Casey quietly.

They followed the professor back to the second-floor room. Keenan wouldn't let go of the man in the homburg until the office door was closed.

"I'd like to show you my identification," said the man calmly. Carefully he pulled an official-looking wallet from his pocket.

"Captain Hill, State Department," moaned Ralph after he took a look.

"Oh, boy," sighed Keenan.

"We're sorry, sir," said Sasha. He handed Captain Hill his hat. "I saw the two of you meeting before."

"I know, I know. You suspected the work you were doing was being used against your country." The captain smiled. "I guess we did look pretty suspicious."

"I didn't want to explain any more than I had to, Sasha," explained Professor Casey. "I was told to keep you in the dark. No one was to know what the codes were for."

"I told you they were codes," said Keenan triumphantly.

"Yes," continued the captain. "We're using the equations as part of our submarine communications. They're very important."

He turned to Sasha. "There was some question about not using a U.S. citizen to complete the work. But Professor Casey assured us of your outstanding skill and your loyalty to your new country."

"But who is Rottweiler?" asked Sasha.

"What?" said Professor Casey.

"I found this note in your office," explained Sasha. He pulled the slip of paper from his pocket and showed it to Professor Casey.

"That's my dog," laughed the professor. "My wife has a poodle named Rottweiler. I was supposed to pick him up at the vet that day."

12

River of Freedom

It was the first warm evening of spring. A sprinkling
of white blossoms peered out of the swollen buds on
the cherry trees. The grass no longer crunched
underfoot.

Sasha strolled across campus. He was heading toward the New Haven Green. Church bells chimed from one of the little churchs' tall steeples.

He had completed the coding equations for the week and would deliver them in person. He spotted the man wearing a homburg sitting on a park bench.

"Good evening, Sasha," said Captain Hill.

"Nice night," Sasha replied. He sat next to the captain.

Sasha handed over the work.

"You're getting even faster," complimented the captain.

"Thanks. They do have a certain pattern. You might want to think about adding more variables. If I can see the pattern, there's a chance that the enemy might too. It's a bit like fencing. You can't be predictable," said Sasha.

Captain Hill nodded. "Let me know what you have in mind. I'll show it to the folks upstairs. You're doing important work here, Sasha." He pushed back his hat.

Sasha nodded. "Will we win, sir?" he asked.

The captain hesitated. "I don't know yet." He rubbed his hands over a weary face. "I don't think even Roosevelt knows. The Pacific is a mess." He sighed.

"One thing I do know is we'll never give up," said Sasha.

Captain Hill smiled.

"I have something for you," said the captain.

"What?" asked Sasha.

"Professor Casey explained your situation. As part of your background check, I had to investigate your family," the captain said. "I know you've been trying to find out about them for several years."

"There's been no news in almost two years," said Sasha. "Most of the time, I just try not to think about it." He shrugged. "There's nothing I can do."

"I have a few contacts," said the captain. "They found someone who works in the Resistance. He seemed to know you. His name is Derek, no . . ." The captain searched in his coat pocket for an envelope.

"Dieter?" whispered Sasha.

"Yes, that's it," agreed the captain.

"Here. He wrote you a letter. I'm afraid it's not all good news," said the man. He handed a small plain envelope to Sasha.

"But at least I'll know," said Sasha.

Captain Hill tipped his homburg. He walked off into the spring darkness.

Sasha pushed the buzzer insistently. He prayed that Vida was home. Sometimes she worked the second shift at the factory.

"I'll just wait," he said to himself.

"Yes. Who is it?" rasped the voice over the apartment's intercom.

"It's Sasha. Is Vida home?" he shouted into the speaker.

The apartment door buzzed. Sasha dashed up the two flights of steps to Vida's apartment. Maryanne opened the door.

"What are you doing here so late, honey? Vida's asleep," drawled Maryanne.

"I know. I'm sorry. It's very important," said Sasha breathlessly.

"Sasha," said Vida coming out of the bedroom. "What on earth? It's after midnight." She tied her pink robe around her waist.

"I borrowed Ralph's car and begged gas ration coupons from everyone. I have news," explained Sasha. He held up the envelope.

"About your family?" asked Vida excitedly.

"I'll make coffee," suggested Maryanne. She disappeared into the kitchen.

"I knew I had to be with you when I opened it," explained Sasha. "It may . . . it may be bad news."

"Come sit with me," said Vida. Sasha sat next to her on the tattered sofa. "Open it when you're ready."

Sasha stared at the envelope for a moment longer. Then he broke the seal. He didn't care that Vida could see his hands shaking. He unfolded the single sheet.

April 1942

Dear Sasha,

So much has happened in Latvia since you left. When we last spoke, I realized who I had become. I was not very proud of what I did. When the Russians came, I joined a Resistance group.

At first I was safe in Riga. But after the Germans invaded, we were forced into the countryside. I must not say more.

In the weeks after the Russians took over, we all thought that somehow things would be the same. Then the soldiers began to round up people. George, your sister's husband, was among the first. Our best guess is that he was shipped to Siberia.

Thousands of Latvians were forcibly relocated in the next few months. I tried to find out about George for Raisa, but there was a wall of silence. Raisa may have been spared because she was Russian.

Then, last June, Hitler double-crossed Stalin and invaded Latvia.

Do you remember where we last spoke — St. Peter's Tower? I watched it burn to the ground that day. Great blackened holes are all that are left. The German bombers destroyed the bridges and the port as well. What the Germans missed, the Russians destroyed as they retreated.

Raisa was in the old town shopping when the bombers came over. We could not find her after.

Sasha hesitated. "I don't know if I can read any more," he whispered.

"Take a moment," comforted Vida.

Sasha could only nod. Then he read on.

Poppy and Larik were at home and were not hurt.

Sasha let out a huge sigh. He didn't try to hold back the tears. He continued reading, gathering strength as he read.

I have some relatives in the south of Latvia. I took Larik and Poppy there to stay with them that day. They will hide there as peasants until the war is over. It was the best I could do. You know that Poppy will protect Larik.

I'm so glad that you and Ralph are away from this. We did have some good times. Whatever you do, don't come back. Find a way to fight this from where you are. You were right. You should not be a part of it.

If you see Ralph sometime, tell him I'm glad he's safe. I'm afraid there's little hope for his father. After the Germans came, most of the Jews were sent to Poland.

> *Your friend,*
> *Dieter*

In the morning, Vida and Sasha took a walk along the Charles River in Boston. The sun was shining, but Sasha couldn't feel its warmth. Small sailboats ducked under the Longfellow Bridge.

Sasha's heart ached in his chest. Nothing seemed to ease the pain.

Vida said quietly, "It will get better, Sasha. The pain will lessen. I know."

Sasha tried to smile at her. "Raisa was so beautiful, so good to me. But bombs don't care, do they?"

They wandered through the narrow streets. Vida took Sasha to see the old North Church.

"Have you heard of Paul Revere?" she asked, still trying to cheer him.

"He was the one who rode to warn the colonists about the British army, right?" asked Sasha. "That was the beginning of the Revolution. I learned that in my first American history course this year."

"This is where the lanterns were hung. You know. One if by land, two if by sea," Vida explained.

"So this is where freedom started," said Sasha. He gazed up at the tall thin steeple on top of the small church.

"Well, it started many places. Philadelphia was where the Declaration of Independence was written. But this is where the battles started. Lexington and Concord aren't far. Across the river is Bunker Hill," Vida pointed out.

"Those people fought hard for their freedom," she continued. "They sacrificed a lot."

"They all did what they could so that we could be free," agreed Sasha.

They had walked out to the point where the Charles River flowed into the harbor. Larger ships were moored at the piers. The spring breeze rippled past. Sasha caught a faint whiff of spring mixed with the salty sea.

"Do you miss Keenan?" asked Vida.

"Yes," answered Sasha. "But he was so happy when he left. I couldn't feel too bad. We all have to do what's necessary to win this war. We must fight just as they did."

"What will you do?" asked Vida. "Will you join and fight?"

Sasha could see the fear in her eyes.

"Sometimes there are things you can do at home that are just as important," he told her.

"So you won't have to go away?" she whispered.

"No," said Sasha. "I am where I belong."

Epilogue
1969

Sasha had checked the flight schedule three times in the last five minutes. He tapped his watch. Had it stopped?

"Relax, dear," said Vida. "It will only be a few more minutes."

He smoothed back his hair nervously. It had recently begun to gray a bit at the temples.

"This wait seems longer than the last 35 years," complained Sasha.

"Flight 78 from Moscow now arriving," called the voice over the loudspeaker.

Through the wide windows of the airport, Sasha studied the people as they came down the steps from the plane. A gush of people flowed in from the double doors. Sasha searched, hoping he would know the face.

A small woman with silver hair and clear bright eyes entered the waiting area. She searched the crowd. Then she made her way to him.

"Sasha," was all she could manage.

Sasha folded her into his arms.

"Mama," he whispered.

"I kept my promise." She smiled.

"I knew you would," Sasha said.

Author's Note

The books *River of Ice, River of Amber,* and *River of Freedom* are based on real people. The stories have been fashioned around the truth with other fictional characters added. Great care was taken to surround these characters with true accounts of the history of the time.

Sasha is my dear father-in-law, Victor Lazare. He left his mother in Moscow and was smuggled out of Russia with his grandparents at the age of eight. He did not see his mother again until 1969. She was finally allowed to leave Moscow for a three-month visit. During her long career as a medical doctor, she was punished with two years in the gulag.

After his father died, Victor lived with his sister, Raisa, and nephew, Larik, in Riga until he was 17. Her husband's name was Boris.

In 1940, Boris was forced by the Soviets to Siberia near the Ural Mountains. Raisa disappeared during the bombings of Riga. Larik was rescued by his nanny. They hid for the rest of the war in the Latvian countryside. Larik was eventually reunited with his father and grew up in Siberia.

Victor would have participated in the Olympics of 1940. They were canceled when the Soviets attacked Finland.

Victor came to America in 1939 and learned to speak English. Then he attended Yale University, where he studied chemistry. He did help his math professor with encryption formulas. His roommate's name was Keenan, and they were on the fencing team together.

Victor met Vida, a girl from Illinois, after World War II. She was a widow with a small boy. Her first husband, Don, had died as a fighter pilot during the war.

Victor's friends in Latvia did not emigrate with him. All other characters in these books are completely fictional.

Thank you, Vida, for encouraging me to write this story.

Glossary

Arizona   one of the battleships that was bombed at Pearl Harbor

blitzkrieg a war conducted with great speed and force

bout a fencing match

Branford College one of eight residential colleges at Yale University in 1942. Students lived in small apartments with one or more roommates. They ate in a common dining room and shared other study rooms. A master lived in the college and helped with studies and problems. The college was built in a square with one large and two smaller courtyards.
Students belonged to one college for all four years of school.

director   the head umpire in a fencing match. He analyzes the action, polls the judges, and awards the touches.

Dunkirk a major French seaport that was attacked by Germany in May of 1940

embassy   the headquarters for a country's official representatives

encryption secret codes used during the war to protect information from enemies

epee a fencing weapon with a triangular blade and a larger guard to protect the hand. Touches are scored with the point, and the entire body is a fair target.

feint a pretend attack that distracts attention from the real attack

fletch an attack in which a fencer launches himself at his opponent very quickly, attempts a hit, and then passes at a run

foil a fencing weapon with a 35-inch rectangular blade and a small guard to protect the hand. Points are scored with the covered tip of the foil only on the torso of the opponent.

Harkness Tower a stone tower at the corner of Branford College. It is square at the bottom and octagonal at the top.

Hirohito the emperor of Japan during World War II

Hitler, Adolf the leader of the Nazi Party in Germany during World War II

homburg a man's felt hat with a stiff, curled brim and a high crown creased lengthwise

Latvia a small country in Europe where Sasha lived with his sister before coming to America

lunge to thrust the body and blade forward

GLOSSARY

Moscow the capital city of Russia

Nazi the German party that controlled Germany under the leadership of Adolf Hitler

New Haven Green a large square park in the center of New Haven. Homes and businesses still face this open area. Three small churches were built on the green.

on guard the position fencers take when ready to fence

parry to block an opponent's attack

Riga the capital city of Latvia

riposte to attack immediately after a fencer has blocked an opponent's attack

Roosevelt, Franklin the president of the United States during World War II

salle a fencing hall or club

Siberia a region in Russia where political prisoners were sent

Stalin, Joseph the leader of Russia during World War II

touch a point scored in fencing by touching the opponent with a fencing weapon

touché the expression used to acknowledge a touch by a fencing opponent

M